This book is to be returned on or before
the last date stamped below.

Being Brilliant

Acknowldegements

Thanks to: Colin Salter for helping think through the original idea;
Sue Concannon for the constant pep talks and the inspirational words
– 'They can't sack us until after the inspection,' is classic motivational
stuff; Ann Bullock for giving me lots of rope but not quite letting me
hang myself; Jackie Rawling for understanding me; JC, Steve 'The
Legend' Kay, Sally, Cliffster, Mr Seymour, Andy Whittaker and all
the other excellent trainers I've been associated with for the past
five years; all at Loughborough College; David Hyner for use of the
goal-setting pyramid and for general all-round 'good guy' stuff; Ed
for making it all happen, so damn quickly. Brilliant.

First published in 2006 by Balloon View Ltd
Regents Place, 338 Euston Road, London NW1 3BT

This edition published in 2006

Edited by Jo Kemp

Designed and set by Barbara Linton, London W13 8DG (020) 8997 0337

Printed in Great Britain for Balloon View Ltd by Stroma Ltd,
Unit 12, Commercial Way, Abbey Industrial Estate, London NW10 7XF
(020) 8961 5407

Balloon View Ltd
Regents Place
338 Euston Road
London NW1 3BT
www.balloonview.com

Being Brilliant

By Andrew Cope

balloonview

The author

Andy Cope is a professional trainer, qualified teacher, author and learning junkie.

His background is in retail management, but he has spent the last few years in adult education, teaching full time at Loughborough College and occasionally at the Universities of Leicester and Derby.

Andy is reluctant to bite the hand that feeds him but is concerned that too much of the academic world is shrouded in nonsense. 'There are too many theories, big words and models that nobody understands. Even if you do manage to fathom the complex thinking, the learning has no impact.' His personal bugbear is when lecturers trot out management thinking from 20, 30 or 40 years ago. 'A lot of it is just not relevant to the modern world of work. Maslow's Hierarchy may be good stuff but if I see it again, I'll scream!'

This frustration with academia has led Andy to set up a business that is focused on influencing people to think differently. His flagship course, 'The Art of Being Brilliant', has been delivered to excellent reviews in businesses and schools throughout the UK and South Africa. 'The focus is on translating some of the highbrow academia into clear, simple messages that everyone can take on board.'

Andy has worked with many corporate clients and believes that the messages are equally applicable whether you're on the shop floor or in the boardroom. 'The Art of Being Brilliant' is for anyone who has a passion to make the most of the raw materials they've been given. The underlying message is blindingly simple. 'Why settle for anything less than being yourself, brilliantly?'

Andy is married to Louise. He lives in a small town in rural Derbyshire, surrounded by fields and silence, although quite often the silence is broken by their two young children, Sophie and Ollie. Andy is also a keen football fan and supporter of the very unfashionable Derby County. He doesn't have much spare time but when he does he loves to read, write and listen to music.

Andy is also a children's author. He has penned the highly successful 'Spy Dog' series. The first book won the Red House Children's Book Award for 2006 and he is currently working on book four of what is to be a five-book series.

Andy runs in-company leadership programmes as well as a series of open workshops. If you would like more details please visit www.artofbrilliance.co.uk or email Andy direct at andy@artofbrilliance.co.uk

Contents

Section 1: The curtain raiser

Section 2: The performance

Section 3: The encore

Section 1:

The curtain raiser

A very important beginning...

There are more books on leadership and management than I wish to count, never mind read. Some are dreadful, most forgettable and only a handful inspirational. You can generally glean one or two nuggets from each, but I wanted to write a book that contained enough nuggets to set you up for life. After all, what would you rather have, an occasional golden egg or the goose?

Modern organisations, whether public or private sector, big or small, rely on *people* for their competitive advantage. The world has moved on and so must your workforce, yet many are worn out by change. Let's face it, work is exhausting – life is exhausting! Change has not only crept up on us, it's mugged us and left us battered and beaten. Change is also a thief. It steals your time and robs you of energy. What's more, nobody's arrested it, so change is free to run amok in society, business and the community. The bad news is that change is a repeat offender that we are going to have to get used to.

The good news is that we can fight back. New management fads and fashions come and go, but what is here to stay is the centrality of people to organisational performance. If your people are at a low ebb, your business will at best limp along and at worst disappear. If your people are average, your business will also be run-of-the mill. If your people are brilliant then, guess what, you have a fighting chance of surviving the next few years. There are no guarantees, but you may even prosper and grow.

The burning question, therefore, is how can we get our people to be brilliant? How can we ensure that every employee works to the absolute maximum of his or her potential? How can we help them to be inspired all day, every day?

The answer lies within leadership. *Being Brilliant* is a simple story about a circus. It explores issues of modern leadership, albeit from a slightly quirky perspective. It examines how we can think and behave differently in order to inspire those around us. If we acquire the habits within this book, the effects will reverberate throughout our working and personal lives. We are not trying to motivate people from 9 to 5, we are seeking to inspire 24/7 and transform the lives of others by first transforming our own.

However, before we begin in earnest, let's look at what this book *isn't*. It starts with the raw materials that make up 'you' and makes no pretensions about transforming you into a film star, professional footballer, supermodel or astronaut (unless the raw materials are already there, of course). It doesn't guarantee to turn you into a millionaire. There are no promises to make bald heads spring into bloom and it can't cure illnesses. In short, it can't turn you into something or someone you're not.

So now we know what this book isn't, can we pinpoint what *Being Brilliant* is? The principle is remarkably simple. In short, *Being Brilliant* is about working with the raw materials that you've been given and making the most of what you already have and who you already are. It's about creating new positive habits and losing some of your undesirable ones (particularly thinking habits, such as negative thought patterns). *Being Brilliant* is about a new, improved version of you. It's about learning to live at the upper reaches of your potential. Most of all, it's about how brilliant you can be when you put your mind to it.

The book delves into cutting-edge business issues such as positive psychology, transformational leadership, appreciative inquiry, emotional intelligence and neuro-linguistic programming, without getting bogged down in academia. Textbooks are full of theories we don't really understand and big words that we instantly forget. We don't need big words, we need clear messages that we can apply easily.

Leading by inspiration

Forget 'leading by example'. It's OK up to a point but has some serious side effects. For example, I know lots of managers who take pride in working long hours because 'it sets a good example'. One in particular used to boast about being the first in the car park in the morning and the last out at night, as if this automatically made him an excellent manager. Far from it; it just proved that he worked long hours. All he actually achieved was to make his staff feel guilty for leaving the office on time and daring to have a life outside work. He didn't actually inspire anyone with his presence and it was quite a relief when he wasn't around. We could relax, be ourselves and be productive.

I knew another who made sure she could do all her team members' jobs to prove her worth to them. 'Respect' was her watchword. 'I won't ask them to do anything I can't do myself,' she boasted. All very laudable but what was the result? She spent so much time doing their jobs that she never actually 'managed' anything at all. Her team was totally reliant on her expertise. As a result, they bothered her with every little problem and while she became stressed out, they forgot how to think for themselves. 'Leading by example' meant she became bogged down with trivia and her team lacked motivation and direction.

I'm not saying that 'leading by example' is necessarily a bad thing, just that the modern leader needs more. I believe the elusive ingredient is 'inspiration'. So, supplement 'leading by example'

with 'leading by inspiration'. Now you have the ingredients for a mouth-watering leader that the modern workplace craves. This is someone whose presence inspires you to give your best, day in, day out, during good times and bad. They don't necessarily know exactly what you do or how to do it themselves, but they do spend time talking to you. They want to know your ideas for improving performance. They listen, coach and praise. They are calm under pressure. They laugh, sometimes even during the bad times. They have high expectations and you raise your game to meet these. You feel valued and you love your job. Most importantly, you grow.

Someone who 'leads by inspiration' can achieve all of the above and, boy, what a difference it makes to morale and performance. Unfortunately, these are the rarest of individuals. In my career to date, I have had many managers who have lead by example. I've respected their knowledge and hard work and have done well for them. But I've only ever had one manager who has led by inspiration. And guess what? She didn't work long hours and couldn't do my job. But she did coax me to levels of performance that I had no idea I was capable of. She helped me grow. It's only now that I realise she was what academics would call 'emotionally intelligent'. She made me feel that I was capable of great things and gave me the confidence to go for them.

I believe we can all change. I also believe we can all learn the fundamentals of 'emotional intelligence'. I'm certain that if we apply the principles we can learn to be brilliant. By this, I mean we can all make changes to the way we think and behave that will bring about better results from the people within our sphere of influence. What's more, it has little to do with academic ability and everything to do with attitude.

Let me give you another example. Recently, a friend of mine confided that he thought he was a shoddy parent. He held his hands up to being irritable and impatient with his children. He admitted to working long hours, partly because of the pressures of work but partly because his three young children meant that home life was very demanding. He confided (with a tangible sense of guilt and disappointment) that it was easier to be at work than at home. He was brilliant at work, thriving on the pressure and rising to the challenges. The lull started when he got home. 'I get home at half seven and the kids descend on me,' he grumbled. 'They want me to go outside for a game of football and all I want to do is sit down, watch TV and have a cup of tea.' And he's by no means alone in this mindset. I don't blame him – life's exhausting. The easiest thing in the world is to sit down and relax in front of the TV, especially after a hard day. There are times when we *need* to sit down and relax, but a semi-permanent existence in front of the TV is hardly being brilliant. We know we can do better but we are drawn into a comfort zone of habits, many of which don't serve us well at all. The easiest thing in the world is to fall into an 'average' mentality. Let's face it, 'average' is what most people are most of the time. Average parents sit and watch their children playing rather than joining in. Average managers spend their time on emails rather than with their people. Average comedians make you smile instead of laugh out loud. Average books make you skip bits rather than devouring them from cover to cover. Average lives slip by with a whimper rather than a roar. Average is everywhere and the easiest thing is to settle comfortably into it.

But I knew that if my friend changed his attitude he would see the situation differently and could therefore choose a different response. He just didn't realise that he had a choice about how he felt. If he stopped to ask himself why his children throw themselves on him the minute he steps through the door he might perceive the situation differently. It's simple – he's their dad, they love him. He's the focal point of their world. My advice was to appreciate coming home to three loving children, because these joys don't last forever. Throw yourself wholeheartedly into life, whether it be work or parenting. He's not going to get a second chance at being the best dad he can be. Let's face it, in a few years the children will be teenagers who couldn't care less whether their dad is home or not!

Brilliance isn't *what* you think, it's *how* you think. This book is about the 'whole you'. The lessons to be learned from *Being Brilliant* are as applicable to your home life as they are to your career.

The theatre of life

Recently I read a great piece of advice:

'Live in the front row of your life – participate.'

Its brilliant simplicity stopped me in my tracks. Ask yourself this – if life's an auditorium, where are you sitting right now? If you are sitting somewhere comfortably in the middle or towards the back of life's great theatre (where, let's face it, it's safe and nobody takes too much notice of you), then it's time to change. Sitting in the front row of your life doesn't mean you have to be loud, pushy or extrovert. It's not about trying to be someone you're not. It means that you take charge of your life, know yourself, assert your confidence and challenge your comfort zones. It's about being the best version of you that you can muster – and being it consistently. Sitting in the front row is about making things happen.

Lately I've *consciously* moved from the safety of the back row towards the front row of my life. I put consciously in italics because I, like you, had a choice. My four major breakthroughs were:

1. appreciating that this is the only life I'm going to get, and making the decision to go for it (and enjoy it!)

2. realising I have a choice about the version of me that I am (i.e. back, middle or front-row 'me')

3. realising that I can take positive action that will help me move towards the front row of my life

4. taking (and sustaining) that positive action.

Point 1 is a no-brainer. Your life is accelerating away. You probably feel like it's going on around you. If you're anything like me, days, weeks and months are zipping by in a blur. So why not start to appreciate them?

Point 2, realising that you have a choice about the version of you that you are, is more challenging. It may be that you are perfectly happy sitting in the middle or towards the back of life's theatre. Many people argue with me on this point, saying they are fine where they are, thank you very much. I don't have a problem with this. Frankly, if they want to be 'fine' then that's their choice. All I'm saying is that they can raise their game to 'brilliant' by thinking differently. 'Fine' is a comfort zone. To me, it implies complacency. My point is that you get a much better view and are able to participate much more from the front. Life's too short to sit at the back. If you don't believe me, try this: imagine it's your 100th birthday and someone asks you how your life's been. You reflect for a second, put on a watery smile and reply, 'It's been fine, thanks.' Is that good enough for you? If so, read no further. This book is not for you!

Now imagine it's your 100th birthday (again!) and someone asks you how your life's been. You look at them with a sparkle in your eye, a beam on your face and say with genuine passion, 'It's been absolutely brilliant, an amazing journey, thanks.' The difference between 'fine' and 'brilliant' is cataclysmic, but there are positive actions you have to take NOW for your life to be brilliant.

Point 3 is about taking this positive action. You can only take positive action if you understand where you are now and where it is that you want to be. For many people this can be very challenging because they don't have anything specific they want to achieve. They don't know where they want to be. Most of us drift through life. We end up doing what we do through chance rather than any grand design. And the bad news about positive action is that it takes energy, effort and commitment, which is why 98% of the population are content to sit towards the back of life's great theatre.

If you feel strongly enough about points 1, 2 and 3 then point 4 follows automatically. You will take positive action. Sustaining it depends entirely on how badly you want positive results. If you don't feel strongly enough, the pull from the back row will be irresistible and, after an initial spurt, you will eventually return to your comfortable seat towards the back of life's great theatre. Remember, this is where most people are sitting, simply because it requires the least effort. The easiest thing is to join them. When I run my 'Art of Being Brilliant' workshops, I follow them up with a session six months down the line called 'The Art of Staying Brilliant', just to check that the new habits are self-sustaining.

So, commit now to taking charge of the only person you can – you. It's a marvellous experience. My challenge to you is to read *Being Brilliant*, apply its principles and make life happen for you rather than around you.

Comfortably numb?

The diagram below is a good place to start your new thought processes.

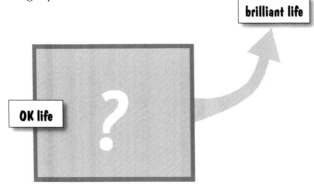

Consider for a moment what lies inside the blue box. What is it that can transform us into brilliant individuals? When I ask this question in my 'Art of Being Brilliant' workshops, people often say that money is inside the blue box. It's a fair assumption that if you won the lottery it would transform (and very probably improve) your life. It would make you rich and possibly very happy, but would it make you brilliant? Does the latest plasma screen TV create a life-changing experience? When you die, will they talk about your plasma screen TV? I doubt it. They are much more likely to talk about *you* – your character, personality, habits and their memories of you. Cash is superficial but brilliance lies much deeper. The message to be learned from *Being Brilliant* is achingly simple: *you* are inside the blue box – the choices you make, your passion for life, your attitudes, the relationships you build and the memories you leave.

Consider this sobering thought. An average life span gives you approximately 27 000 days. You may be lucky and get a few more or unlucky and get a few less, but we average out at around 27 000. A big number? Not surprisingly, the answer largely depends on your perspective. When I run a workshop in schools, teenagers leap out of their chairs in excitement because 27 000 days seems like forever. Yet, ask the same question of a corporate audience and I'm often greeted with a collective gulp. All of a sudden it's not such a massive number. I can see vexed faces, their brains working overtime, calculating how many days they might have left!

The crucial factor is how you react to this not-so-groundbreaking news. You can panic and get thoroughly depressed. Or you can be inspired. 'What?' I hear you cry. 'How can I possibly be inspired by knowing I have only 27 000 days, especially as I've already used up a fair few?' Let me ask you a painful question. How many days have you already wasted being less than brilliant? The reason I ask is that the 'old' me used to waste them by the hundred.

To get an inspirational, life-changing response I prefer to focus on the future. How many more of your precious days and weeks do you want to waste being anything less than brilliant? What impact would you have on your family, friends and work colleagues if you made the conscious choice to be yourself, brilliantly? How can you make the right choices? And, crucially, how can you sustain being brilliant? We need to wake up and get a grip of life in order to maximise our 27 000 days. Let me make this perfectly clear – the life you are leading isn't a practice, it's most definitely the real thing. If you spend a day being anything less than brilliant then that day has been wasted. You aren't going to get it back, it's just another notch on the great bedpost of life. Try to think of life, and emotions in particular, as being like a boomerang – if you're being 'average' then you are likely to get 'average' thrown back at you from your work colleagues and children. This is the easiest route to take and is as comfortable as your favourite armchair. But 'average', just like your favourite armchair, is a comfort zone. You settle into it, night after night, having the same conversations, watching the same TV programmes, your days ticking by. If you can raise your attitude and thinking to 'brilliant', then 'brilliance' is likely to be reflected in those closest to you. This is more difficult than being yourself 'averagely' and requires more passion and energy, but is far more rewarding. My, what a powerful choice you have. Not only can you change your life but you can also have an inspirational effect on everyone around you, most notably your children. And you can change today!

As a teacher of management/leadership I hear lots of people making excuses for their lack of brilliance, blaming just about everyone except themselves. Fingers are often pointed at senior managers, teams, colleagues, customers, suppliers, family and 'circumstances'. When I ask, 'What are the barriers to you being brilliant?' you need to think for a moment and then turn the finger and point it back at yourself. More often than not, the answer lies within. This book is not about making excuses; it's about taking responsibility.

15

What follows is a carefully crafted story – Alfonzo's story. It takes place in a circus, but I'm hoping you will realise that it isn't really about a circus at all, it's about you. It's about the pressures of modern life, such as the stresses and strains of combining the dual roles of career and parent. For many, this is a delicate balance. And an exhausting one. Follow Alfonzo's trials and tribulations carefully. His leadership style is flawed and he makes the same innocent mistakes that we all do.

Each chapter has a review section where you are asked a series of questions that reflect on what you have learned. Crucially, each chapter also has a challenge. These challenges are specifically focused on positive actions you can take – right now – to improve some of the most vital aspects of your life. If you read *Being Brilliant* and ignore the reflections you will merely be entertained. Contemplate the questions and you will be enlightened. Complete the challenges and you will be transformed!

The story has an epilogue in which the themes are brought together and explained a little more academically. This serves two purposes. Firstly, it means that those readers who prefer big words don't feel cheated. And secondly, it encourages readers to learn about some of the more modern aspects of leadership thinking.

And finally, before the story begins, consider this book an investment in yourself. Enjoy it for what it is – a very simple pick-me-up, a thought-provoker and an antidote for those who are irritated by the slowness of the microwave, become impatient in the fast-food queue, are annoyed with the time it takes for their computer to boot up and don't have enough time for their loved ones. If you are exhausted by 21st-century life, this book is for you and about you. It comes with the perspective that you are unlikely to inspire anyone else unless you are first inspired yourself. Remember this very simple message: you don't have to try to be anyone else, just be yourself, brilliantly. It's the most powerful choice you have.

Let Alfonzo's story begin.

Section 2:

The performance

Episode 1:

The first steps to being brilliant

'Just picture it. The big top full to bursting, the audience taking their seats, murmuring in excited anticipation of the best show they'll ever see. They've heard it's an awesome event and have come along to see if Alfonzo's Circus really *is* the best show on earth. You enter the main ring, dressed to the nines. The crowd falls silent; the spotlight picks you out like a ray of sunshine on a cloudy day. You stand a moment, looking around at the children's beaming faces and adults' breathless anticipation. You are the consummate professional, soaking it up, milking the moment, letting the atmosphere build. You wait until the crowd falls to a hush. Then, chest out, arms aloft, you bellow your welcome to what will be an extravaganza of the senses. You ooze confidence, born from the fact that you know that what's about to happen is a well-orchestrated spectacle, bringing the finest performers together in a show that will dazzle each and every paying customer. You know that they will leave breathless, hurrying home to tell their families, friends, neighbours and workmates about the performance. It is breathtaking. Your job is easy – the ringmaster to a finely honed team of performers. Close your eyes and imagine it. Smell the greasepaint, listen to the gasps of amazement, live the passion, see the excited faces, feel the emotion...'

The ageing impresario rose wearily from his chair. He could take no more. 'Enough lad!' he barked. 'Will you shut that big mouth of yours. That's the biggest load of claptrap I've ever heard. I don't know what planet you're on but look around you. What do you see? Go on, open your eyes and take a good look. You're describing a circus as it used to be, probably one from some book you've read or film you've seen. This ain't a bleedin' fairytale – it's real. My job is to get this ramshackle bunch of losers to perform six nights a week plus Saturday and Sunday afternoons. You've never seen such a bunch of deadbeats in all your life. "The greatest show on earth?" Get real. The only applause we get is a slow handclap, and the best bit's at the end when the punters get off their backsides and clear off home.'

Bruno the Acrobat considered the outburst and the demeanour of the ringmaster. The big man was weighed down with anger and frustration. His shoulders sagged as much as his overhanging belly. As the ringmaster wiped his forearm across his brow, Bruno considered that everything must be an effort for him. The ringmaster sweated a lot. The sweat was brought on by the stress of keeping the circus going, maintaining any sort of audience for a show that had been run into the ground. The plain fact was that the world had moved on but Alfonzo's had stayed still. Come to think of it, as Alfonzo often did during sleepless nights, the show hadn't stood still at all, it had gone backwards. Sure, he had recruited some new acts, but these only partly filled the gaping holes left as his established performers walked out. One after another, starting with a trickle, then a flood, performers threw in the towel. His best juggler was now an IT technician, his knife-thrower worked on Tesco's meat counter, his plate-spinner worked in a Greek restaurant and his Indian rubber man was diversity manager at the local council. As Bruno had described the tumultuous scene, the ringmaster imagined he was there with him, every step of the way. If only... But painful reality had brought him back down to earth faster than a trainee tightrope walker.

Alfonzo had the circus in his blood. He was a fiercely proud man, but there is only so much that a manager can take. He'd seen the good days, he'd lived Bruno's vision, but that was in the past. Customers nowadays had more choice for how to spend their leisure time. Alfonzo's Circus was competing with theme parks, multiplex cinemas, trendy pubs, snow domes, nightclubs, bowling alleys, laser shoot 'em ups, waterparks – all state-of-the-art attractions designed to squeeze leisure income from his punters. The plain truth was that expectations had risen and circus standards hadn't. Audiences had plummeted and Alfonzo acknowledged that he had allowed the once magnificent circus to run down to its present ramshackle state. Despite his best efforts the acts were second rate: the clown wasn't funny, the juggler couldn't catch, the contortionist had a bad back and the knife-thrower's assistant was off 'with her nerves'. He had an acrobat who was scared of heights and a fire-eater on long-term sick leave with a bad throat and singed eyebrows. The animals were lovingly looked after but Alfonzo had had to cut back because of the animal rights movement. The health and safety executive were investigating his lion tamer and the elephant trainer had packed it all in because of the risk-assessment paperwork. The vehicles were old, the wagons in need of repair, morale broken and the magic well and truly gone. Even the big top itself had three gaping holes, so sections of the audience were issued with umbrellas in case it rained. Alfonzo's shoulders slumped further as his mind wandered. How long could he maintain the circus as a going concern? His life's work was trickling away, his enthusiasm ebbing with it.

He considered the young man, the visionary, the Fancy Dan in front of him. He probably knew nothing about circuses. He was another trainee acrobat, probably like all the others – a 'traveller' who could do a few somersaults, assuming that he could make it as a star. Fat chance. Not at this place. He would be like all the rest: start reasonably well, get trained up, then become fed up and leave. They always did, especially the good ones. He'd probably end up working in a factory.

The ringmaster inhaled deeply and blinked back tears of frustration. 'Still, the show must go on,' he said, half-heartedly. 'Get off to your training and if you're any good, we'll give you a slot next week.'

Bruno the Acrobat stayed put. Alfonzo glared at him from beneath his shaggy eyebrows, his feisty ringmaster bravado returning. 'Go on, Fancy Dan, buzz off and do something useful.'

'I intend to do something useful,' replied Bruno calmly. 'With your permission, I'd like to be given the opportunity to help turn this place around. I want to get this circus back to being the greatest show on earth.'

24

Alfonzo wasn't often lost for words. It usually only happened when the human pyramid collapsed in a heap, or the knife-thrower drew blood, when he was so angry at their incompetence that words failed him. But this was different. There was something calm about this lad. Something assured. Alfonzo continued to glare at Bruno, but was met with warmth. The big man softened. 'Tell you what, lad,' he chuckled, 'if you can turn this nightmare around you can have it – tent, animals, caravans, the bleedin' lot. What are you, some sort of head case? Let's face it, if your job is to swing from trapeze to trapeze at fifty foot, then you've got to be mad. We don't get many acrobats who are management consultants you know.'

Bruno maintained an air of defiance. 'I'm not a consultant, I'm a believer.'

The ringmaster erupted into laughter. 'You don't say. A believer eh?' he mocked. 'What is it, a religious thing? Don't go all evangelical on me. A believer. Now I've heard it all.'

The acrobat smiled confidently. 'It's not a religious thing. I'm a believer in people. I'm a believer in me and a believer in you.'

Alfonzo found himself lost for words for the second time in a minute. A million thoughts passed through his mind, none of them triggering the words he wanted. 'A believer in me,' he echoed, voice trailing away. The big man sank back into his chair, incapable of coherent speech. He just loved the words. 'A believer… *in me?*'

'Yes. This place can change, but only if you do first.'

'Me? You cheeky little so-and-so. I'm not the problem round here,' boomed Alfonzo, pleased that his bravado had returned. 'It's the rest of 'em. It's that manic-depressive clown for a start, and that cocky idiot of a lion-tamer. In fact, I don't think I've got a single performer who hasn't caused me sleepless nights. So, lad, I'm not your problem, in fact I'm the only one holding it together. Go ask 'em.'

'Is that so?' enquired Bruno, nodding sagely. 'Have you got a few minutes to think things through with me?'

The ringmaster, normally full of bluster and feigned aggression, felt calm. He took a deep breath and considered all the jobs he had to do. Last night's show had gone particularly badly yet they still had three more nights in this godforsaken town. Somebody had to go into the city and sell tickets. Who was going to pick up the litter and fetch the diesel for the generators? Then there were the animals to exercise. He had promised to go and see Curly to talk through a possible new clown routine and then there was Chippy and his bad back. So many things to do, yet Alfonzo felt relaxed, calmed by the young man in front of him. 'Aye, lad, a few minutes won't make any difference. What thinking do you want me to do?'

'I want you to think about you – nobody else – just you.'

Alfonzo furrowed his brow and ran his fingers

through his thinning hair. 'I've already told you, it's not me that's the problem.'

'I know what you've told me, but please just listen and think. Keep an open mind and give me five minutes of your time.'

The big man considered for a second. He didn't normally have time to stand around chatting, there was simply too much to do. But he'd promised a few minutes, so what the hell. 'Fair dos lad, go on then. I'll try and keep my beak shut. But you'd better be quick because I can't keep it buttoned for long.'

'OK, well we've already closed our eyes and seen the vision of what this circus *can* be,' Bruno reminded him.

Alfonzo's frustration boiled over again. 'Yes, but that was a vision, a dream, not bleedin' reality. Closing my eyes and seeing it doesn't make it happen, does it now lad?'

The trainee countered with his customary unflappable manner. 'Please, Alfonzo, listen. Don't just hear – listen. You say you're not the problem. It's the customers, right? And the performers and the animals and the way they don't work together. It's the lack of skills and training. It's attitudes. It's everything. Am I right?'

'Now you've got it lad – yes, it's absolutely everything. That just about sums it up,' conceded the big man, furrowing his brow and reaching for a hanky to mop the sweat away.

'Who's in charge around here, Alfonzo?'

'I am, of course,' proclaimed the ringmaster in exasperation.

'And who recruited the performers?'

'I did, of course,' boasted Alfonzo, stabbing a finger into his chest.

'Who trains them?'

'Well, me I suppose,' said the big man, a little more slowly.

'And Alfonzo, tell me who sets the mood of the camp as it travels from town to town?'

'Me… well no… all of us actually. But me mostly.'

'Who pays them and looks after their welfare?'

'Me again.'

The acrobat nodded in agreement. 'And finally, Alfonzo, who truly inspires them?'

Alfonzo seemed lost in thought. 'Probably not me,' he conceded eventually. 'They're difficult to inspire, see. I get the best out of them by being me. Some I cajole, some I have to bellow at. They know what they've got to do but they're just not up to it.' Alfonzo disappeared into his thoughts for another moment. 'And anyway, what do you mean by "inspiring" them?'

'I like to think of inspiration as "lighting the fire *within* someone rather than under them",' replied Bruno.

'Lighting the fire *within*,' trailed Alfonzo in his usual way. 'I suppose,' he considered, 'that I probably light the fire under them. You know, show them who's boss, throw my weight about a little. We're all grown ups here you know and they can be a pretty rough bunch. Give 'em an inch and all that.'

'And what reaction do you get when you light the fire *under* them?'

'Well, they always do what I tell them,' smiled Alfonzo, jabbing a fat finger into his barrel chest.

'Interesting. And do they do *more* than you tell them?'

Alfonzo's brow furrowed again. 'Whaddayamean, *more* than I tell them? Why would they do that?' he asked quizzically, as if the idea was completely insane.

'Do they help you pick up litter? Do they come into town and help sell tickets? Do they muck out the animals? Do they relax in your presence? Do they come up with ideas? Do they invite you round to their caravan for a beer?'

Alfonzo was still sceptical and countered, in his usual blunt manner, 'OK, Smart Alec Acrobat, what exactly do I have to do to light their fires *within*?'

'Lots of things,' said Bruno. 'What I'm really talking about is changing you from 'leading by example' to 'leading by inspiration'. The first thing is to recognise that you are part of the problem. You must realise the extent of the impact you have on those around you. You will affect everyone with whom you come into contact, you have no choice about that. However, you do have a choice about whether it's a positive or a negative impact. Think about this. There are people who, when they walk into a room, can light it up with their presence. They haven't said or done anything except enter the room. There is something about them that makes others feel emotionally brilliant. I bet you can think of someone.'

Alfonzo nodded. 'That's easy – Jamie, our previous fire-eater. He was awesome, sort of lifted everyone just by being around. Can't put my finger on it exactly because he wasn't actually very good at fire-eating, kept burning his mouth. Once he even inhaled instead of exhaled and ended up in casualty! But he had a sort of presence. He was good to have around. He packed it in to become a teacher and we miss him badly.'

Bruno nodded and continued, 'Yet the opposite can also be true. I bet you can think of people who can enter a room and shift the mood downwards. No words are spoken but the atmosphere is worse for their presence. Emotionally, people feel disheartened and downcast. I call these people 'energy vampires' – they suck the energy and passion out of people. They leave you feeling unenthusiastic, as if you're just going through the motions – they certainly don't inspire. My question to you Alfonzo is, in your heart of hearts, which person are you?'

Alfonzo instinctively knew the answer but mulled it over. He eventually conceded, 'Energy vampire probably, not all the time like, but probably for the best part of most days. But it's circumstances that make me that way. I'm under a lot of pressure. And anyway, so what if I am an energy vampire?'

'You, Alfonzo, are the acknowledged leader of this circus. Agreed?'

'Agreed.'

'Well, in any social interaction it's the leader who has the biggest influence on the prevailing mood of the team. *You* set the tone. Everyone takes their cue from the leader, whether it's in an office, factory, family or circus!'

Alfonzo thought for a second. 'So if I cheer up a bit, that will influence others to be a bit more cheerful? That's hardly rocket science is it, my bendy friend?'

'No, it's not difficult,' agreed Bruno. 'The question is, Alfonzo, if it's not difficult to do, why aren't you doing it?' The acrobat acknowledged the big man's shrug and continued. 'Most people don't make the choice to be positive and upbeat. They don't even realise they have a choice. They end up drifting through life being average or below, having some good days but mostly bad...'

Alfonzo couldn't resist butting in. 'But I'm not a cheerful person. You're asking me to be something I'm not.'

The acrobat was ready for him. 'No, big fella. I'm not asking you to be anyone else, I just want you to

31

be yourself, *brilliantly*. If you are, the results will follow. You can turn this place around, but first you need to have a good hard think about yourself and what I've said.' Bruno studied the big man for signs of understanding but was met with a vacant stare.

'Tell you what, we can get started right now. Give me six words that describe you on a good day. Six words that describe how you feel when you're ten feet tall and bullet proof. Six words that describe you at your brilliant best.'

'Hell fire, it's been a while since I've been at my brilliant best, lad,' chuckled Alfonzo, his face breaking into a craggy smile revealing the almost forgotten laughter lines around his mouth and eyes. 'Let me think… well, passion for a start. I used to have a passion for life, still do I suppose. And energy, I always have bags of energy on a good day. Enthusiasm… happiness… and what about drive? I used to have bags of that.'

'Great, that's five. Give me one more,' encouraged Bruno.

Alfonzo stood tall and expanded his barrel chest, enthusiasm showing in his body language. 'Passion, energy, enthusiasm, happiness, drive and… and… brilliance! There, that's six. Great words eh? The words themselves make me feel awesome, like the old me.'

'Great, but they're not just words, they're feelings and emotions. I'll call them your "six-pack". Who's in charge of your six-pack, Alfonzo? Who's in charge of you feeling brilliant?'

Alfonzo's face lit up again as the penny dropped. 'I bleedin' well am,' he beamed. 'Do you know what, I am lad,' he repeated, letting it sink in for a second time.

'And if you make the conscious choice to embrace these feelings, what effect will it have?'

'On me or everyone else?'

'Both.'

'Well, I'll feel brilliant and I suppose I'll start to make those around me feel pretty good too. I'll be the one who can light up the room rather than darken it. You know what lad, I'll be able to light fires within!' Alfonzo was struck with the simplicity of what he'd just said. 'Leading by inspiration…' he mused. 'Holy mother of Jesus, I've been an energy vampire all these years. I'm a big part of the problem round here and from now on things are going to darn well change. Just watch me go.'

'OK,' said Bruno, 'but don't get carried away. Remember, things will not turn around overnight, there are more lessons to learn.'

'Happy to learn them. Can we do it now?' persisted the big man, buoyed by the positive endorphins buzzing through his body.

'This has to be a step-by-step approach,' explained Bruno. 'I want you to think about your attitude and emotions for the next 14 days. I want you to make the choice to live your life according to the words you chose for your six-pack. Alfonzo, I am setting you a 14-day challenge. You must simply go away and be *you, brilliantly,* for 14 consecutive days. If at any point during that time you find yourself reverting to the old Alfonzo, you go back to day one – it has to be 14 *consecutive* days of brilliance. Then, my friend, your choice of feelings has become a habit and we can continue. Deal?'

Alfonzo leaped from his chair, spat on the palm of his hand and offered it to Bruno, who shook it warmly before surreptitiously wiping his hand on his trousers. 'Deal! We have an agreement my friend. See you in 14 days' time!'

Lesson 1

Think about the attitude you display to others and be aware of the choices you have. You can choose to inspire those around you, or you can choose to demoralise them. Now you know you have a choice, exercise it carefully.

Questions to consider

1. Imagine being yourself brilliantly. What do you look like (general appearance, facial expression and body language)? What kind of things does the brilliant you do and say? What do people say about the brilliant you? How does the brilliant you approach life? How do you approach problems? What does it feel like to live life as the brilliant you?

2. What's stopping you being brilliant?

3. How do you want to be remembered? Write a paragraph that sums up what you want people to say about you when you're not around.

4. What changes do you need to make? When do you intend to make the changes?

Challenge 1

Create your own six-pack (go on, I know you've always wanted one!). Choose six feelings that you would like to feel more often and write them down. Carry them around with you and read them until you've learned them. Use your words to create energy and monitor how you feel.

Consciously choose to feel brilliant for 14 days until your new feelings become a habit

Episode 2:

Staying brilliant

Twenty days later…

'Hell fire, lad, you never told me it would be so difficult.'

Bruno smiled knowingly. 'So, Alfonzo, being yourself brilliantly for 14 consecutive days was trickier than you thought?'

'Tricky? More like bleedin' impossible. It's other people that get me down. That excuse for a clown for a start. Never met a more miserable waste of space in my whole life. I bounced into his camper the other night and there he was, in tears, saying he couldn't remember his lines and that he was worried about getting the routine wrong. Said he needed someone to buddy up as a double act. In fact, said he needed a troupe of clowns! So I said, 'Pardon me, Mr Hilarious, but that's the best joke I've heard from you in a long while.' Before I knew it we were bellowing at each other like we always do and I was back at day one of my 14-day challenge. The miserable swine spoilt it for me.'

Bruno sighed knowingly. 'No, Alfonzo, you spoiled it for yourself. Let's go back a step. Who's in charge of your six-pack of feelings?'

'Well I am. But you can't legislate for miserable individuals like Mr Bleedin' Face Paint,' spat Alfonzo, his blood pressure heading north once again.

The acrobat remained calm. 'OK, so Curly spoiled your mood. He spoiled your day. So who won?'

'Who won?' shouted the ringmaster victoriously. 'I let him know who's boss if that's what you mean.'

The acrobat fixed Alfonzo with his gaze. 'I didn't ask you who's the boss and I'm not interested in who shouted the loudest. I asked you who won.'

'Who won?' repeated the ringmaster, this time more quietly and slowly, as if actually considering the question. 'Well, he did I suppose. He made me feel angry.'

Bruno breathed a sigh of relief. 'He only made you feel bad because you *let* him. Remember the energy vampire thing? It boils down to emotions. As you entered his trailer, you felt great and he felt terrible, right?'

'Right.'

'Two minutes later, as you left the trailer, you both felt terrible. Right?'

'Spot on.'

'So, yes, you're absolutely right, he won. He won because in that situation he was emotionally stronger than you. He was the energy vampire and you let him win. He infected you with his negative emotion. You probably let him ruin your whole day. Tell me Alfonzo, what happened after you left his trailer?'

The ringmaster pondered for a moment. 'Well, I stormed out, naturally, and went back to Mary and the kids. Oh, and on the way I bellowed at the new apprentice tightrope walker because she was nattering instead of practising. Shouted to her that she would end up as hopeless as all the rest if she didn't get her backside in gear. Then went back to my caravan and told Mary what a bunch of deadbeats we had to put up with. Shouted at her and the kids actually, more in frustration than anything.'

Bruno pondered momentarily, allowing the information to sink in. 'OK, so Curly had infected your mood and you had allowed that to pass to the other staff as well as your family. The clown had got you in an emotional embrace. What you've just described is a typical example of how contagious emotion is.'

Alfonzo was pensive for a moment, his face etched with thought. 'Mmm, so that means Mr Face Ache had dragged me and my family down. And he didn't even *meet* my family. His mood passed to them through me, the devious so-and-so. How could I have handled Curly differently?'

'You tell me, Alfonzo,' challenged the acrobat.

The big man gave it considerable thought. There was silence in the camper van, broken only by the monotonous metal on metal of tent pegs being hammered into the turf outside. 'Suppose I shouldn't have shouted,' he offered eventually. 'Then he wouldn't have shouted back. I wasn't being brilliant, was I?'

Bruno nodded. 'Keep going. How would a brilliant Alfonzo have handled the situation?'

The ringmaster continued to think out loud. 'I suppose if I'd stayed positive, you know, kept the six-pack at the forefront of my mind, I could have influenced him upwards instead of him influencing me downwards. The whole situation would have had a different outcome.'

'Well said,' congratulated Bruno. 'Try and think in terms of outcomes more often. It often helps to think of *trigger, feeling, behaviour* and *outcome*. In this case the trigger was Curly and you chose to feel angry.'

Alfonzo shook his head vigorously. 'No, he *made* me angry, I didn't choose to be. It just happened.'

The acrobat failed to disguise his frustration. 'It "just happened" because you didn't consciously make a choice about how you felt, and your default emotion in that situation registered you as angry. You only ended up angry because you didn't *think* about the choice of feelings you have.' Bruno took a deep breath before continuing. He took a step towards a nearby table and knocked on it loudly with his knuckles. 'Hear that my friend? This table is a real object. It is actually here in front of us, visible and solid.' Bruno knocked again to make his point. 'But what goes on in your head isn't real. It's made up. *You* have created it. Do you get my meaning? If you want to, and know how, you can create good feelings and emotions rather than anger and frustration. We're back to making choices, Alfonzo.

It's a very powerful skill.' The acrobat paused to gauge if anything was sinking in. 'Let me give you an example, OK? Imagine that someone cuts you up in traffic. Let's say they pull into the queue at the very last second. How do you feel?'

Alfonzo furrowed his brow. 'Angry, obviously. I mean, it's so frustrating when that happens. I've abided by the rules and then some idiot cuts in at the last moment. My blood boils and I usually end up driving two inches from their bumper to show my anger.' Alfonzo had gone red in the face at the thought. 'Sometimes I give them a few hand signals as well,' he growled. 'If you know what I mean!'

'Fine,' nodded Bruno. 'But you need to understand that it wasn't the bad traffic that made you angry.'

'It wasn't?' asked Alfonzo, looking puzzled.

'No. It was how you *thought* about it that caused your negative feelings. It was how you processed the information. And, with a bit of practice, you can learn to process information differently – more positively. What other feelings could you have chosen in that road rage situation? Think for a minute, big fella.'

The ringmaster nodded silently as he ran through the scenario again. 'Well,' he ventured, 'I guess I could have laughed it off. I could have said to myself, that poor bloke, I wonder what pressure he must be under to have to get to work six feet earlier.' After a pause, Alfonzo's creased forehead flattened out. 'Tell you what,' he said brightly, 'I could just turn my CD player up and sing. I don't have to feel angry at all!'

Bruno clenched his fist at this breakthrough and quickly followed it up. 'So, back to Curly. He was the trigger for you feeling angry. Your behaviour turned to shouting and the outcome was awful – just a continuation of the bad relationship. Imagine the same trigger but with different feelings, behaviours and outcomes. Remember, it's your choice. Close your eyes and tell me what would have happened if you had *chosen* to feel differently. Go on, replay it in your mind.'

Alfonzo did as he was told. 'OK, well I'm walking into Curly's camper and he's in tears, moaning about his act, in other words, same trigger as before. Instead of feeling angry I have *chosen* to feel encouraged that he wants to improve his performance. I guess it stems from him wanting to do his bit of the show better. Between us we could have seen the opportunity to improve, chatted it through and I would have felt great. We could have talked through some ideas, cheap ones mind, and had a go. No tears, no shouting. I would have left the trailer, having had a nice cuppa, gone back to my family and said what a great bloke Curly was. I'd have been smiling, wouldn't have shouted at Mrs Tightrope or the missus.'

Bruno nodded encouragingly. 'And Curly?'

'He'd have felt great too I suppose. Tears replaced by excitement. I would have inspired him. What did you say last time we met? I'd have "lit the fire within".'

The acrobat gave a big thumbs-up. 'Exactly. So, let's start again. Who spoiled your mood?'

42

'I did!'

'And who's responsible for you being brilliant?'

The ringmaster eventually conceded, 'I am, OK. But what about energy vampires? You know, there are people around here who just refuse to be happy. They seem to actually get a kick out of being miserable. How can I change them?'

'You can't change them. You can only change you,' replied Bruno matter-of-factly.

The ringmaster looked puzzled. 'I can't change them? What do I do then, just avoid them?'

Bruno shook his head. 'Listen carefully, my friend. What I'm about to say is very important. Firstly, most people aren't genuine energy vampires, they will respond almost immediately if you are on good form. What were your six words again? Energy, enthusiasm, happiness, drive, passion and brilliance? Your influence will be almost instant. You'll feel great and this will transmit to others, especially since you are the leader. But, true, there are people who are more difficult to influence, folk who seem to find joy in being downbeat about life in general and work in particular. These are dangerous people to have around because they lower the tone of the whole place. Remember, if we give up on them, they've won! There's a very simple strategy for dealing with energy vampires. Firstly, don't let them lower your emotions to their level, otherwise they win. Hold your emotional high ground. Remember, if you have chosen to feel brilliant then it's your responsibility to maintain that level. Remain positive and upbeat – remember the words from your six-pack. This will keep you buoyant. Secondly, over time, begin to influence them upwards, towards your level of emotional brilliance. This won't happen overnight but, if you are consistently on good form and have consistently chosen a positive attitude, they will be forced to feel great in your company. They represent the ultimate challenge for you. If you can emotionally embrace an energy vampire – and win – you know you're moving in the right direction.'

The acrobat saw that the ringmaster was nodding enthusiastically, so pressed on. 'Most people are easy to influence – if you're positive, they will be; if you're happy, they are more likely to be. This, my friend, is your next challenge. I want you to positively influence every person you come into contact with for the next 14 days. Make them feel great. Inspire them, Alfonzo. But, of course, this only works if you genuinely feel great first. Remember, we're not able to change anyone – but we can *influence* them, massively. In fact, the truth is that we have no choice *but* to influence them, so we may as well make our influence positive. I'm talking about everyone – work colleagues, family and friends. You can become brilliant to be around.'

Bruno walked over to the nearby flipchart and picked up a marker pen. He drew two straight lines across the board, labelling one 'upper level of positive' and one 'lower level (negative)'. 'Let me share some simple research with you.'

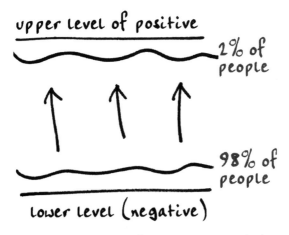

upper level of positive

2% of people

98% of people

lower level (negative)

'The upper line represents how great you *can* feel during the day. Your high points. You know, when things are going really well. This is perhaps how you feel after a brilliant performance. You feel alive, energetic and passionate about life.' Alfonzo nodded and the acrobat continued. 'The straight line at the bottom represents your low point of the day. This is how you feel when things go wrong, or if energy vampires impact negatively on you. For example, if the show hasn't gone so well and the customers complain. You feel lousy. Low energy, no enthusiasm, can't be bothered?' This time Alfonzo was nodding more enthusiastically, as if he understood this end of the scale much better.

'I'm going to share some messages from positive psychology with you,' explained Bruno. 'What if I told you that more than 98% of people go through their days existing at a much lower level of happiness than they are capable of?' Bruno ran his finger along the bottom line. 'They exist here,' he said, drawing a wavy line towards the bottom of the scale. 'Life is exhausting. The pressure of work and family life is immense. They get through each day, having survived it, hoping that tomorrow may be better. Ninety-eight per cent of us count down our days to the weekend or to our next holiday. Ninety-eight per cent! That's *most* people, Alfonzo. We come alive on Fridays because the weekend is nearly here.'

The ringmaster remained in a pose of nodding silence as if this made perfect sense.

'What I'm saying is that these people are normal. They are in the vast majority. Look around you and you see them all the time. Life is happening around them. I'm interested in the top 2%, those who live each day here,' Bruno continued, running his finger along the upper line. 'These people have the same pressures as everyone else but they think differently. They bounce through their days feeling great. They are positive, passionate, optimistic and energetic.' The acrobat drew a wavy line just below the top of the scale of happiness. 'However, nobody has ever studied these folk because they don't have "problems". But I'm very interested in their way of thinking. What if we could learn to think how they think? What would happen?'

Alfonzo had added wide eyes to his silent nodding. 'You mean if we lived life in the upper range of how great we could feel, instead of down in the doldrums? It's dead simple,' he gaped, reaching for a purple marker. 'I guess we could move from here to here,' he said, drawing upward arrows. 'We could *choose* to live at the upper end of our scale of happiness,' he added enthusiastically. 'We could even learn new habits of thinking that would keep us there.' The ringmaster smiled at the apparent simplicity of it all, before a frown descended on his face. 'But I can't feel fantastic all day every day – nobody can. It's not normal, is it? Besides, someone will punch my lights out for being too cheerful. I'll get people thinking I'm on funny pills, or worse!'

The acrobat took a deep breath and suppressed his frustration. 'Alfonzo, we're back to choices. *You* decide how you feel. You can make the choice and tell your brain about it. Your brain then tells your body and your body will respond to the chemicals your brain releases. If you make the choice to feel fantastic, your face will smile, your brain will release positive chemicals and you will feel a surge of energy. You can, of course, make the choice to feel awful,' explained Bruno, running his finger along the lower line of the diagram. 'Your brain will respond and your body language will follow. You will not only feel terrible but you will be lousy company. It's a simple choice and that's the *whole point*. Many people don't make any conscious choice about their feelings at all. They exist on autopilot. Their moods are a lottery, often descending into average, sad, stressed or angry. You often hear people saying that they feel great because it's Friday. Or you ask them how they are and they say, "I'll be all right at 5 o'clock." Loads of people get that Monday morning feeling, sometimes from Sunday lunch onwards: a sense of impending doom. These people are putting off fun and enjoyment until after work. Why? Why not choose to feel great all day, every day? Life is so full of choices that it's bewildering.

One choice you've already decided to make is to run this circus. You can run it with a grim look on your face or you can choose to be awesome. The ball's in your court. Remember, Alfonzo, you spend a seventh of your life on Mondays, so don't be miserable about them!'

Bruno paused for breath and watched for Alfonzo's response. 'Let's take this a bit further. Tell me something you really enjoy doing – something that makes you feel alive. Tell me about times when you are here,' he said, running his finger along the upper level of happiness.

'That's easy,' replied the ringmaster. 'As a family we're pretty much tied to this place day after day, week after week. It's difficult to get a holiday. But every year, around February, we make an effort to go abroad, somewhere sunny, where I spend time with the children and actually switch off. I feel marvellous, energetic and completely relaxed.'

'And your attitude when on holiday?'

'Oh, just total brilliance, being away from everything.'

'OK, what if I told you that the activities we do are neutral. Whether you're sunning yourself in Spain, sitting here in your caravan or are out there performing – the activities themselves don't matter. *You* are the constant feature of all those activities, so what if you chose to bring your holiday emotional brilliance to the circus?'

Alfonzo took a few seconds to digest the fact that he

could choose to have a brilliant attitude at work.
'Brilliant attitude…' he began, 'at work? Holy smoke
sonny, I'd be awesome,' said Alfonzo, wide-eyed,
imagining the impact. 'But, I've tried and I can't. It's
more difficult than you think. Life's so fast and
there's so much to cram into every single day. Can't I
be down here just a little?' he asked, pointing to the
lowest line on the blackboard.

A note of exasperation crept into the acrobat's voice.
'That's the whole point. It's *your* choice. If you want
to be unenthusiastic about life, go ahead and be
depressed – it's a free world. But before you do, let's
do some maths. How old are you, Alfonzo?'

The big man's body sagged. 'Fifty-bleedin'-two,' he
mumbled as if it wouldn't matter so much if he said
it quietly.

'OK, let's say you're going to live to be 90.'

'With my blood pressure – no chance,' smiled the
big man, patting his chest.

'The new you has much lower blood pressure,'
explained Bruno, 'so let's stick with 90.' The acrobat
closed his eyes tight for a moment, screwed his face
up and scratched his head. Alfonzo resisted the
temptation to speak. Eventually Bruno opened his
eyes and unfurrowed his brow. 'That leaves you 38
years, which is, by my rough calculation, about
13 000 days.' The acrobat paused for effect. 'How
many of those do you want to waste being
miserable?' Alfonzo's eyes widened but no words
were forthcoming, so Bruno continued. 'And
remember, when you're miserable you're

emotionally locking your wife and children into being miserable, so you're robbing them of valuable days too.' Bruno paused again, letting the ringmaster think about his wasted days. 'Of course, it's all about balance. Everyone is allowed to have an off day – it's called "being human". And maybe it's not appropriate to be happy every day of the week; but I'm not talking about being perennially happy, I'm talking about choosing to feel as good as the situation will allow. For example, it would be inappropriate to be happy at a funeral or a disciplinary interview, or if you were ill. Consider it as positive rather than happy, although the two are quite closely related. We all have bad days, but we can minimise our miserable time and, with practice, eliminate it completely. That, Alfonzo, is the "art of being brilliant".'

Bruno sensed that the big man was half convinced. Alfonzo inhaled deeply while he considered everything he'd just heard. 'Mmm. Sounds easy although I know it isn't. But just imagine the reaction I'd get from other people if I did make the right choices. This is really simple, right? You're basically saying I can *choose* to be positive.'

Bruno opened his duffle bag and pulled out a folded piece of paper. 'Have a look at this,' he said, handing it to Alfonzo. 'Come and see me when you want to speak some more.' The men shook hands again and, for the first time, Bruno saw a spark in the ringmaster's eye.

The big man strode purposefully back to his caravan, chest out, positive gait and a big smile on his face.

As he marched past, the trainee tightrope walker looked up and stumbled off her low rope, collapsing into the cushions below. Alfonzo grinned at her. 'Awesome my girl, truly awesome. You keep practising and one day you'll be our headline performer. You have got real star quality.'

The girl looked at Alfonzo and then at her trainer, beaming delightedly. A grin spread across her trainer's face too and he encouraged her back onto the rope. Alfonzo felt brilliant as he entered his motor home. He beamed at his wife and flicked the kettle on. He unfolded the piece of paper and read.

The Importance of Change

When I was young and free and my imagination had no limits, I dreamed of changing the world. As I grew older and wiser, I discovered the world would not change, so I shortened my sights somewhat and decided to change only my country. But it too seemed immovable.

As I grew into my twilight years, in one last desperate attempt, I settled for changing only my family, those closest to me, but alas, they would have none of it.

And now, in what will probably be my final year, I suddenly realise: if I had only changed myself first, then, by example, I would have changed my family. From their inspiration and encouragement, I would then have been able to better my country and, who knows, I may have even changed the world.

Anonymous
Written on a tomb in Westminster Abbey

51

Lesson 2

Practise living in the upper reaches of your range of happiness and stop blaming others when you're having a bad day. Take control of the only person you can – you! If you genuinely feel brilliant you will positively influence those around you.

Questions to consider

1. Consider how often you are an energy vampire. Ask yourself (honestly) how often you talk negatively, have a less than positive attitude, grumble, blame other people or sigh.

2. When your attitude is below par, what effect do you have on yourself and others?

3. Think of the worst energy vampire at work. How do they make you feel?

4. When you feel like that, who's won?

5. How can you change your attitude and/or behaviour to influence people's mood upwards?

Challenge 2

Close your eyes and imagine the worst
energy vampire in your life –
a person who really irritates you or gets
you down. Make the picture as clear as
you can, then add their voice. Listen to
what they are saying.

Now, using your imagination, give them
some Mickey Mouse ears. Add some
tufty pink hair and a clown nose. Dress them in a
polka-dot toga and put a sign round their neck that
says, 'Beware of the energy vampire'. Make their voice
high and squeaky, as if they've been inhaling the gas
from a helium balloon. Imagine that all they're saying is
'blah, blah, blah'.

When they seem really silly and trivial, make the
picture smaller. Turn it black and white. Shrink it to the
size of a postage stamp. Imagine a dustbin. Open the
lid and put the picture in it.

Next time you meet this person, imagine them as
above and smile. They're not worth worrying about.
Don't let them win.

Challenge 3

Lock horns with someone who's grumbling, and win. Make sure their mood softens rather than yours hardening. Talk positively. Turn their negative into a positive. Praise their work, consult them on something or ask for their expertise, being sincere in your positive attitude towards them. Monitor how you feel and assess how they might be feeling after an encounter with a brilliant you.

Episode 3:

Creating positive relationships

Three days later, Bruno emerged from the shower to find Alfonzo ensconced in his caravan kitchen.

'Hi, my flexible friend,' grinned Alfonzo. 'Can you spare me ten minutes? Kettle's on.'

'No problem,' replied Bruno as he disappeared into the bedroom to dry off. The two men continued the conversation, with Bruno in the bedroom and Alfonzo in the kitchen. 'How's things?' shouted the acrobat.

'Do you know what, I feel absolutely fantastic,' enthused Alfonzo, stirring the tea.

Bruno grinned to himself. He could hear the ringmaster smiling as he talked and knew the big man would be beaming from ear to ear when he saw him. Sure enough, as Bruno pulled on his shirt and walked into the kitchen, he was met by Alfonzo's warmly lit face, with colour in his cheeks and a sparkle in his eyes. The laughter lines were back and the body language had changed. 'You're looking great,' admitted Bruno.

'All thanks to you, my friend,' gushed Alfonzo.

'Not true,' replied a cryptic Bruno.

'Oh yes it is. Without our little chats I'd still be the miserable so-and-so of a few weeks ago. I've changed big time. Everyone's beginning to notice, especially the wife!'

55

'Let's go over this again shall we,' encouraged Bruno. 'Who's changed?'

'I have,' proclaimed the proud ringmaster.

'And who's responsible for you being brilliant?'

'I am. Nobody else, just me,' asserted Alfonzo proudly.

'So I haven't changed you at all – you have.'

Alfonzo was a little disappointed to be wrong-footed yet again. 'Erm… well yes, if you put it like that. I've done the changing and, you know, it's the best thing ever. I'm on day 12 of my 14-day challenge. I wake up, have about ten seconds of being miserable and then the attitude kicks in. I give myself a good talking to, sometimes out loud, and run through the six-pack with myself. I think passion, energy, happiness, enthusiasm, drive and brilliance. I tell myself that I don't want to waste today being anything less than completely brilliant. Then it's a smile on my face and I'm ready to face the day.'

'Excellent Alfonzo, you have come a long way.'

'Aye, and it's all down to you… well maybe me… perhaps both of us! I was kind of wondering if there was anything else I should know? I've come this far but I bet there's more you can teach me.'

Bruno pursed his lips and stroked his chin. 'I've tried to create an environment where learning can take place,' he explained. 'But the responsibility to learn is entirely yours. So far you've taken the responsibility and accepted the challenge.'

Alfonzo's eyes sparkled. 'Give me more challenges, son. I'm alive to your ideas, alive like I never thought I would be.'

'OK,' said Bruno. 'Do you want to try something a bit more radical? I think we've built the foundations for you being brilliant, but you now need to explore some deeper issues. For example, what do other people think of you?'

'Well, I think they like the *new* me,' enthused Alfonzo. 'I'm great!'

'But you've only been the new you for a few days. You spent the previous three decades being an energy vampire, so there's a lot of ingrained perception that needs to be changed. Come and stand here next to me.'

Alfonzo put his mug of tea on the kitchen table and sidled anxiously over to Bruno. The acrobat guided the big man gently by the shoulders and turned him to face the length of the living room. 'Think of someone you work with, someone with whom you have an uneasy relationship.'

The ringmaster chuckled. 'Right, well, that could be just about anyone. There's Tony, or what about Curly? Boy, have we had our differences over the years!'

'OK, let's take Curly the Clown. Stay open-minded and do as I say. Alfonzo, you are standing here and Curly is ten feet away at the other end of the lounge. Imagine him there. Alfonzo, think carefully and tell me what you see, hear and feel.'

'See, hear and feel,' echoed the ringmaster. 'Erm, well I see a clown, a pretty miserable one at that. Too much face paint, baggy trousers, daft shoes, spinning bow tie. I see him doing a pretty average routine in front of a paltry crowd. I see him making bendy balloons for the kids. I see him being sad.'

'And what do you hear?'

'Hear? Well, I hear him telling the same old jokes and trying to make the audience laugh, which sometimes he does. I also hear him off stage, whinging and moaning about his act and griping about life. He always wants more of everything and doesn't understand the finances.'

'OK,' encouraged Bruno, 'and, looking at Curly standing there in front of you, what do you feel?'

'I feel…' Alfonzo hesitated, 'I feel lots of things. Sympathy, for one. It can't be easy being a clown. I feel anger and frustration because he's not really up to the mark and I think he knows it. I also feel irritation because he doesn't do a brilliant job. The clown should be the centrepiece of the circus. Overall I feel let down.'

'Thanks, Alfonzo.' The acrobat then lead Alfonzo forward ten paces and turned him round. He was now at the other end of the lounge, looking back. 'OK,' said the acrobat. 'Now comes the difficult bit. You are now Curly, looking back at Alfonzo. I want you to be Curly, so clear your head and start to imagine. Looking as Curly at yourself, tell me, honestly, what do you see, hear and feel?'

58

'What do I see, from Curly's view? Well, I see a big bloke, about 50, well probably more like 60 actually, a bit bald, couple of stone overweight, a bit red in the face. Silly 'tash. Smart when he's in the ring but a bit unkempt out of it. I see someone who works hard though. He's always busy.'

'And what do you see him doing?'

The ringmaster took a deep breath before continuing. 'I see him working hard. Shouting a lot, 'specially at me, nitpicking, being aggressive. Picking up litter and doing lots of jobs. I see him introducing me every night. He says the words but I know he doesn't mean them.'

'And what do you hear? What do you hear the ringmaster saying?'

Alfonzo winced slightly before continuing. 'I hear him bellowing at everybody, especially me. I hear him swearing like a trooper. I hear him being stressed. I think he shouts because he's afraid his circus is going down the pan.'

'And, as Curly, what do you *feel* about this man?'

The ringmaster's shoulders drooped and there was a prolonged moment of silence broken by his sigh of resignation. 'Blimey, well, to be honest I feel demoralised. I feel really angry that he shouts at me all the time,' said Alfonzo, sounding surprised at his own reaction. He glanced at Bruno who nodded encouragingly and the ringmaster continued. 'Well, he never listens and that really gets me down. I've got some great ideas and he just shouts them down. I feel just about ready to throw the towel in and if it wasn't for the other performers, who feel pretty much the same, I would have done. Overall, I think I feel frustrated. He's so frustrating to work for because you never know where you stand. He clearly doesn't like me. Do you know what, I think I feel let down too!'

'Thanks, Curly,' said Bruno. 'Now I want you to go and stand on the sofa.'

'Have you lost the plot mate?' enquired Alfonzo.

'Maybe,' grinned the acrobat, 'but please keep an open mind.'

The big man, trusting to the last, took off his shoes and stepped carefully onto the sofa, his feet sinking into the cushions. 'OK,' said Bruno, 'now you are not Alfonzo or Curly, you are just a neutral observer of their relationship, looking down from above.'

'Right,' said Alfonzo, trying to stay with it.

'You have been Alfonzo and know how he feels; you have been Curly and know how he feels. What I want you to do is to look down on the relationship and advise Alfonzo what he needs to do to bring the two closer together.'

'That's easy. The big bloke over there,' he said, pointing to where the imaginary Alfonzo was standing, 'needs to listen a bit more to Curly. He needs to stop bellowing and start listening. If he actually spent more time listening to the funny guy over there they could actually improve their relationship and the act! It would stop the funny guy being so miserable and may even give him the opportunity to be funny. They both want to be great but the gaffer is blocking it. In fact, if the gaffer doesn't stop bellowing and start listening there will be no relationship left.'

'Great,' replied the acrobat, 'and what is the very first thing he has to do to make the relationship better?'

'He's got to listen,' said Alfonzo about himself. 'He's got to really take time out to listen properly.'

'Fabulous,' said Bruno, offering a helping hand as the ringmaster stepped down from the sofa. 'Was that difficult?'

The ringmaster stuck out his bottom lip as he considered the question. 'Er, not really difficult... perhaps a bit scary. I've never really physically stood in someone else's shoes and looked back at myself. I looked, sounded and felt different from what I thought I would.'

'Most people find that,' said Bruno, 'particularly if we examine difficult relationships. The point is that we've created another learning environment. The ball's back in your court again. You can choose to learn something from what we've just done, or you can just ignore it.'

'I really want to improve things, but doesn't he, Curly, have to change as well?' said Alfonzo, jabbing a finger at the imaginary clown. 'There's no point me changing if he stays the same pig-headed misery as before.'

Bruno adopted a look of exasperation. 'Sometimes I wonder about you, Alfonzo! You can't change Curly.'

'I can't?' quizzed the ringmaster, furrowing his brow.

'You can't. But if you change yourself, you may begin to influence him. He has to change himself and he can, with your influence. If you take the advice that you just gave yourself from up there,' said Bruno, gesticulating towards the sofa, 'what will happen?'

'If I listen? Gotcha. This time I've got it. Thanks for the tea, you're a gem.' Alfonzo slipped on his shoes and rushed out into the pouring rain, oblivious, marching purposefully in the direction of Curly's caravan.

Lesson 3

Invest in relationships – it's the only way to keep them strong. Remember, if you don't, someone else will.

Questions to consider

1. Think of someone with whom you have an uneasy relationship (preferably in a work situation). Imagine you are that person. When they're not around, sit in their chair and look back at yourself. What do you look and sound like from their viewpoint? What do they hear you saying? What do they feel about you? Why do they feel like that?

2. What can you do to positively influence their view of you, thereby enhancing the working relationship?

3. When do you intend to start improving relationships and having a more positive influence?

Challenge 4

Take a pen and paper and list ten things that you really appreciate in life but that you take for granted. When you have your list, put a tick by the three that mean most to you (these will probably be people). Appreciate what you have and stop taking things for granted.

Challenge 5

Think of someone you have recently taken for granted (this could be your child, spouse, partner, parent, work colleague, or anyone else). Think about all the great things they do and all the wonderful memories you have. Next time you're with them, catch them doing something really well and praise them. Tell them how much you appreciate them and thank them for being brilliant. Mean it. Make this appreciative behaviour a habit. Monitor how you and they feel.

Episode 4:

Listening for beginners

Three hours later Alfonzo was back at Bruno's caravan, this time displaying an air of frustration.

'Well, my friend, I did everything you said. I chose my attitude and was determined not to let Mr Hilarious get me down and, by and large, he didn't. I sat and listened to him, every whinge and moan about what a sad life he's got. But his ideas are just not affordable.'

The acrobat nodded approvingly. 'What did he say exactly?'

'Get this,' began the ringmaster, 'he said he needed a troupe of at least *six* clowns. He's seen this routine on a film and reckons it'll work for us but he can't do it on his own. I mean, do I look as if I'm made of money? I ask you, six funny faces? I'm struggling to maintain one. He's in cloud cuckoo land. So in the end I made my excuses and left. Didn't storm out mind, I left with my head held high and we didn't get as far as shouting at each other, but we still can't agree.'

Bruno sighed. 'OK, let me ask you again, and this time think about it before you answer. What did he say *exactly*?'

'*Exactly*?'

'Yes, exactly.'

'Well, he said he'd seen a fantastic routine on a film. One that he knew would be brilliant for us and would really pull in the punters. He said he needed six other people to help.'

'Anything else?' probed Bruno.

Alfonzo was pensive for a moment. 'He did mention that Alice might be interested in retraining. Her nerves are shot and she's looking for another skill. And he's spoken with Terry and Petra about them joining in. He reckons they've got time between sets to do the costume changes.'

'So what is he *really* saying?' asked Bruno.

The ringmaster pondered a second. 'He's probably trying to say that he can find and train another five volunteers to take part in the clown stunt – people we've already got.'

'Exactly,' exclaimed the relieved acrobat. 'And how did you leave it?'

'Told him we couldn't afford it – couldn't afford five *new* people that is. But I suppose he knows this and his solution was to train up existing members of the circus. Blimey, I wasn't really listening at all, was I mate?'

Bruno shook his head. 'No, you were hearing. Hearing is easy, as it only requires your ears. It's a very passive skill. Listening is much more difficult because it's an active skill. To listen effectively you need to use your ears, eyes, emotions, intuition, in fact all your senses. You can listen at word level. This is when the words go in one ear and out of the other. You can listen at meaning level, which requires interpretation of words *and* body language. Sometimes the two don't match and the words don't give the real meaning. Or, to be brilliant, you can listen at essence level. This requires you to have an excellent understanding of what makes people tick, a real understanding of human beings. What do the words *really* mean? What is the person *really* feeling? Interestingly, not everyone is naturally good at listening – most merely hear. Others are what I call "emotionally tone deaf", so they can't pick up the subtle social clues that people give off. But, generally speaking, we can improve our listening skills if we try. Let me ask you a question. How often do you find yourself finishing people's…'

'Sentences?'

'Yes, sentences.'

'Erm, probably quite often.'

'Make a conscious effort not to,' advised Bruno. 'Let people finish their own sentences. Give them the respect that their words deserve; it builds rapport and gives you time to really listen, instead of jumping in with a rushed conclusion. In fact, every time you find yourself finishing someone else's…'

'Sentence?'

Bruno gave Alfonzo a knowing glance. 'Yes, sentence. Apologise and encourage them to finish. This makes them realise that what they're saying is

67

really important. And, guess what? They will be more willing to listen to you in return.'

This was too much for the ringmaster. 'But I haven't got time to stand around listening, there's too much to do. And besides, when I ask a question, I already know the answer.'

Bruno smiled sympathetically. 'No, Alfonzo, you know what *your* version of the answer would be. We're talking about tapping into the ideas and inspiration of your staff, not imposing your ideas on them. Tell me, what's been happening to your circus in the last ten years?'

Alfonzo looked crestfallen. 'Going down the pan,' he admitted.

'And who's ideas have you been using?'

Alfonzo looked like a naughty schoolboy. 'Mine,' he mumbled, avoiding eye contact with his mentor.

'So is it a good idea to listen to someone else for a change? What do you reckon? Is it worth *really* listening to your team?'

Alfonzo perked up. 'I suppose this is part of me being brilliant,' he said. 'You know, the new, improved Alfonzo. Positive attitude, a bit of passion for life, leading by inspiration and now a listener too! Tell you what, I'll give it a go. I'll go away and practise listening and report back with my results.'

The two men shook hands and parted, Alfonzo once more striding purposefully out into the rain.

Lesson 4

Practise listening, and I mean really listening, using all your senses. You will be rewarded with respect when it's your turn to be heard.

Questions to consider

1. How good are you at listening?

2. When was the last time you were guilty of 'hearing' instead of 'listening'? What was the result?

3. How often do you listen (and I mean really listen) to the ideas of your team?

4. How can you listen better?

Challenge 6

- Write down three things that you need to do more of in order to create better relationships. Start doing them, consistently.

- Write down three things that you need to stop doing. Stop doing them, now.

Do more...	Stop doing...
1.	1.
2.	2.
3.	3.

Challenge 7

- At your next team meeting, put just one question on the agenda: 'What can we do to be brilliant?'

- Listen to your team's answers and then act on them.

Episode 5:

Creating world-class teams

The circus continued through the summer season.
The atmosphere improved as Alfonzo engaged his
learning. Curly was allowed to try the new routine,
spending hours retraining five colleagues. They
developed the routine until it was spot on and the
clowns became a central feature of the performance.

Autumn was approaching and, with it, the stresses
that a long, hard season places on a circus. Despite
Alfonzo's best efforts, the pressure of touring from
town to town began to take its toll as exhaustion
crept in. The ringmaster coped admirably and
cajoled the performers into achieving hitherto
unattained heights of excellence that surprised even
them. Alfonzo continued to put into practice all the
advice that the young acrobat had given him. He
made enormous strides forward and the atmosphere
around the circus soon began to change.
Attendances began to pick up, particularly when the
word spread about the magnificent troupe of clowns.

Alfonzo felt better in himself. He began to think that
his new positive persona was helping him to work
harder and faster. Every day threw up a new crisis,
but somehow he seemed able to cope. However,
despite his best efforts, Alfonzo still found himself
working up to 15 hours a day, seven days a week. As
the circus season drew to a close, he decided to
consult Bruno once more. This time he intended to
show the acrobat just how far he'd come and was
hoping to pass on some pearls of wisdom to his

mentor. Alfonzo called into Bruno's caravan late one night, after a successful show. The acrobat was making himself a mug of cocoa as Alfonzo knocked on the door. The ringmaster entered the caravan, all smiles, and shook Bruno warmly by the hand.

'Sit yourself down lad,' ordered the ringmaster, 'and I'll share some wisdom with you. I've been doing some reading on positive psychology. It's about time I repaid you in some way.'

Bruno was glad to take a seat and settled into the sofa, mug clasped to his chest, letting the steam warm his chin. Alfonzo, still dressed in his ringmaster's garb prepared himself as if he were about to go on stage. He smoothed his shirt, straightened his hat, pulled his trousers high, cleared his throat and announced triumphantly, 'Life is a jukebox, and do you know what?'

'Nope,' replied Bruno, taking a sip of cocoa.

'*You* get to choose the record!'

Bruno raised an eyebrow and took another tentative sip of very hot chocolate. 'Excellent,' he encouraged. 'What exactly does it mean?'

'It's a self-help thing. You know, similar to what you told me about choosing my attitude. When I'm down I just imagine I'm a jukebox and I can change my mood by playing a different record. Good eh?'

'As I said, excellent. Right now my body's playing "Midnight Hour" by Roxy Music,' said Bruno, glancing at the clock.

'Oh, right,' said Alfonzo, taking the hint. 'And I'm playing "The Show Must Go On" by Queen. While you get some kip I've got another three hours of cleaning up to do.'

Bruno looked surprised. 'You and who else?'

'Just me,' said Alfonzo, sounding surprised at the question. 'Told you, there's loads that I do around here that goes unnoticed. I don't mind, but it does wear me out.'

Bruno glanced at his watch. 'OK, let me pass some advice to you before lights out. How many hours do you work? Twelve? Thirteen? More?'

'More like 15 hours a day, seven days a week,' boasted the ringmaster. 'I still like to lead by example... as well as by inspiration,' he added.

This time it was Bruno's turn to look surprised. 'OK, but these long hours must be taking their toll emotionally and physically. Why don't you ask others to help?'

'Ask others to help?' chuckled Alfonzo. 'I don't think they would. They're paid to perform, not sweep up.'

'Have you ever asked?'

'Haven't liked to, to be honest.'

Bruno looked up from his cocoa and caught Alfonzo's stare. 'But the *new* you is much more respected. Here's my advice and it's going to be quick because I need some sleep, Alfonzo. I know you mean well and you have a lot of responsibility, but please stop living your life as if it were an emergency.'

'What do you mean?' asked the big man, looking momentarily crestfallen.

'Stop rushing around like a headless chicken and start thinking about channelling your energy into what will achieve results.'

The ringmaster went on the defensive. 'I do. Clearing up the litter and fetching the diesel gets results. If those jobs weren't done we'd be in a right pickle.'

'And do you pick up litter brilliantly?'

'No, just the same as everyone else.'

'Well then, I suggest you leave it to someone else and focus your time and energy on what you're really good at, namely improving the overall quality of the performance and getting more bums on seats. Think of "efficiency" and "effectiveness". Efficiency is "doing things right" and effectiveness is "doing the right things". I have a feeling that you are living life as an emergency, trying to do everything properly, but you may be neglecting the jobs that *really* matter, those that will achieve long-term results. I see you being permanently busy, but the circus is standing still, which leads me to think you are being efficient rather than effective. For example, what about getting the hole fixed in the big top or booking the venues for next year? And couldn't you spend some time negotiating discounts rather than just turning up and paying top rent? If you planned ahead, you could get the local tourist information centres to work with you to publicise the circus. That would be an effective use of your time because it would achieve real business results.'

The big man scratched his head. 'Well yes, I see your point but there's so much to do. I haven't got time to plan.'

'Take a deep breath and think about what you need to do to move this place forward.' Bruno paused for effect. 'Go on, do it… a deep breath,' he encouraged, inhaling deeply as if demonstrating.

The ringmaster stood upright and filled his lungs with oxygen before exhaling very slowly, puffing out his cheeks. 'Well,' he said, 'you're right about the tourist information thing. That always needs doing but never gets done. And if the towns were aware, in advance, of us coming we could get some Saturday workshops off the ground, you know, invite the locals to come and have a go for a day. Create some goodwill. And to really move us forward we need to get some sponsorship, especially for the animals. And then there's merchandising and funfair rides. We've talked about it for ages because it sort of complements what we already do, but we never seem to get around to creating the partnerships that would bring it all together.'

'OK, you need to allocate time to these activities or you'll limp along for another season,' suggested Bruno sipping the dregs of his hot chocolate.

'But they're all full-time jobs in their own right,' said the exasperated ringmaster.

'So allocate yourself to them full-time then,' countered the equally exasperated acrobat. 'It will turn you from being efficient to being effective. You need to change the way you think and that will change the way you behave.'

Alfonzo's puzzled expression sparked Bruno into action. 'Well, looks as though I'm not going to get any sleep tonight until you've learned another valuable lesson. Follow me.' The two men left the caravan and made their way to the big top, the diminutive acrobat scampering in front of the striding ringmaster.

Although the hour was late, the trapeze artists were still practising, intent on honing their performance in time for tomorrow's show. Bruno held his hands high, palms stretched towards the agile performers. 'Watch them at work,' he implored.

The acrobats were 50 feet above the ground, two on one platform and three on the other, 60 feet apart. The trio on the right-hand platform held the trapeze.

'OK,' said Bruno, 'how do you think they are going to get from one side to the other?'

'Easy, they're going to swing across the gap,' said the big man matter-of-factly.

'Right, think about a business analogy. There they are now,' said Bruno, pointing to the three trapeze artists, 'and that's where they want to be,' he said, swinging his arm 90 degrees to point at the other platform. 'They know where they want to be, but how are they going to get there?'

'I've told you, they're going to swing. I've seen 'em do it a thousand times, mostly successfully. They tend to practise with the safety net but on the night of a performance they do it without. A bit crazy if you ask me.'

Bruno struggled to hide the impatience in his voice. 'And what does it take to get across?'

'What does it take? Well, skill and ability firstly. I mean, not every Tom, Dick and Harry can be a trapeze artist. It takes practice too I suppose,' said Alfonzo, feeling some learning coming on.

'What else does it take?' persisted the acrobat.

The ringmaster was warming to the lesson. 'Bags of courage, especially when the safety net's not there. And trust… boy, they must have bags of trust swinging like they do. They are totally reliant on each other.'

'They *have* got a safety net, Alfonzo,' said the acrobat cryptically. 'It's called teamwork.' Right on cue, the trapeze artists swung into action. The first one jumped from the platform and swung across the chasm, collecting a colleague from the other side before returning to his partner. Then two trapeze artists set off simultaneously from different sides, somersaulting in the middle and swapping trapezes at the midway point. Whoops of delight were heard from on high as the team congratulated each other.

'Awesome,' said Alfonzo. 'They've certainly got skill, courage and trust. And as you say, they're working really well as a team, you know, helping each other out and encouraging each other to get better.'

Bruno breathed a sigh of relief. 'OK, let's go through those words again. What did you say? "Skill, courage, trust and confidence, backed by encouragement and supportive behaviour, leading to effective teamwork." There's your next lesson Alfonzo, right above you. Apply the principles to the circus generally and what will happen?'

'We wouldn't be far from the vision you talked about all those weeks ago, would we?' beamed the ringmaster, delighted that he'd made the connection.

Bruno had the air of a relieved man, someone who would soon be getting some well-earned sleep. 'You're already getting there I think. Audiences are up, and so is morale. The new you is certainly making a difference, but the challenge is to maintain your positive approach, particularly during difficult times. You need to work out how to build skills, courage, trust and confidence and back it with effective leadership and support. Teamwork will naturally follow. The question is, "What do you have to do to make the next step?" Think about what you need to do to be brilliant. I'm talking about "world class", Alfonzo. Think hard. Now go and do it.'

Before Bruno had finished the sentence, Alfonzo was away, marching purposefully back to his trailer, a plan formulating in his mind.

Lesson 5

Stop living life as an emergency. Spend time reviewing how you work and ask yourself whether you are being efficient or effective. Do the jobs that matter and spend time with your people. Build trust and respect. Work on skills and attitudes. Support with coaching. Teamwork will naturally follow.

Questions to consider

1. How often do you get stuck in the daily grind of work? How often do you find yourself responding to emails and phone calls at the expense of spending time with your people?

2. What would be the benefits of spending time coaching your team and developing their knowledge, skills, attitudes and confidence?

3. When do you intend to start developing your team?

4. What's the first thing to do?

Challenge 8

List your signature strengths (these are the qualities that make you shine). Close your eyes and picture what you look, sound and feel like when you are displaying your signature strengths. Play to your strengths. Focus on making the most of what you do best.

Challenge 9

- Create relationships by being more visible within your organisation. Make a real effort to be visible to people outside your immediate team. You are unlikely to inspire people via email, so reduce your emails by 50% and check them a maximum of three times a day. Increase your efficiency by making all your phone calls in one batch, towards the end of the day.

- Spend time with your people instead. Get to know them better and build positive relationships. Do this consistently.

Episode 6:

Developing people

through coaching

It wasn't only audiences and profits that were on the up. Alfonzo felt rejuvenated. He made sure he chose his attitude each morning and that he maintained his positive outlook throughout the day. He was surprised at the response he got from others and delighted at how he felt in himself. But he was still working long hours, forever rushing around putting things right. When ticket sales were slow he had to conjure up a quick plan to boost numbers; when staff were ill he had to plug the gap; and when the toilet roll ran out in the gents he had to change it. He was the fountain of all knowledge and everyone wanted a piece of him.

Bruno sat and watched as the ringmaster scurried around one Saturday afternoon. First, he was helping to feed the horses, then he spent time in the ticket kiosk, before sprinting to the scene of a spillage to mop the floor. Bruno smiled at the whirlwind of action. He eventually caught up with his boss as he rushed to put out some extra chairs for the matinée performance. 'Hey, Alfonzo, can you stop and chat for a minute?' The ringmaster was sweating from the pressure of doing 25 things at once. He looked at Bruno and smiled. 'I might struggle to give you a whole minute,' he said, 'but for you, I can spare a few seconds. Do you know what? Since our little chats the fortunes of this place have begun to turn around. These extra chairs are for the sell-out audience this afternoon. And we're booked solid for the next four days. It's brilliant.' The ringmaster lowered his stack of chairs, enjoying a moment of rest.

Bruno returned the smile. He took one of the chairs from Alfonzo's stack and sat on it, beckoning the ringmaster to do the same. Alfonzo glanced nervously at his watch. 'But… but the show,' he began, 'it starts in 50 minutes.'

'No "buts", Alfonzo,' soothed Bruno. 'Sit yourself down for a second and watch what's going on around you.'

The ringmaster struggled with one of the folding chairs before eventually perching on it, sitting forward, ready to leap into action. Bruno put his finger to his lips to signify silence and the two men sat motionless as the circus preparation buzzed around them. Performers rushed to and fro, some warming up, some heading for the make-up tent. The food stalls were already busy. Early customers were wandering into the big top to find their seats.

'What do you see, Alfonzo?' asked the acrobat.

'Lots of people going about their business. I see us in the final stages of preparation for a sell-out show. I see nervous energy from the staff and nervous excitement from the customers. It feels great,' reflected Alfonzo. 'But I should be part of it, not sitting here observing.'

Bruno put his hand on Alfonzo's shoulder to stop

him rising from the seat. 'And what's your role in all of this?' probed the acrobat.

'My role? Well, to make it all possible I suppose,' guessed the ringmaster. 'And that means helping out wherever necessary, which right now happens to be putting out these chairs for extra bums to sit on.' This reminded Alfonzo of the urgency of the additional chairs and he stood up. Bruno waved his hands and the big man reluctantly perched once more.

'I agree that your role is to make it all happen. But that's through leadership, vision, energy and passion. What if I said you need to be less hands on and more inspirational?'

Alfonzo was becoming impatient. 'Fair point my friend,' he replied. 'But inspiration isn't going to get these chairs in place, is it now?'

'You'd be surprised,' replied Bruno cryptically. 'Why do you feel the need to do everything?'

The ringmaster fell silent for a moment, in contrast to the hurly burly going on around him. 'Because I'm the boss,' he reflected. 'I've been doing the job for 25 years so I know what needs doing. I'm the one with all the answers. And, at the end of the day, it's my name on the big top and my reputation on the line. I don't think you understand the pressures.' Alfonzo was breathing heavily again, this time through the stress of inactivity.

'I understand the pressure more than you think,' replied Bruno in his usual calm manner. 'But isn't there someone who you can coach in the basics? Someone you can develop? A person you can teach and trust?'

'In theory I suppose,' agreed Alfonzo. 'I mean, Jerry is excellent and I know he's a bright lad. But what if he doesn't want any more responsibility, or, worse still, what if he mucks things up?'

Bruno nodded. 'Have you ever mucked things up, Alfonzo?'

'Course I have,' he smiled. 'Loads of times.'

'And what happened?'

'I learned the hard way I suppose,' grinned the ringmaster. 'You know, things like having a spare generator and spare fuel. Which venues are really soggy and you end up with wagons stuck in the mud. What kind of performers we need and how to avoid hiring dodgy ones who upset everyone else. I've mucked up in all these areas and have learned by my mistakes.'

Bruno continued to nod. 'I think you should coach Jerry. Bring him on. Teach him the ropes. That way he can take some of the day-to-day strain and you can get on with being inspirational. Wouldn't it be useful for him to know about some of the mistakes you've made so he doesn't make them in the future?'

Alonzo considered carefully. 'You're right, I should,' he replied. 'But I haven't got time to sit around coaching him. There are too many other things to do. I can't afford the time.'

'That's a common excuse,' nodded Bruno, 'but not a very good one. Think of coaching and mentoring as investment time. You pay in now, but it repays you with interest later. Like savings, you get back more than you put in, even if "putting in" is a bit painful at the time. And you never know, Jerry might come up with new ways of doing things. He might be better than you!'

Alfonzo shook his head and smiled, 'No chance. He hasn't got 25 years' experience under his belt.'

'Exactly,' nodded Bruno. 'And that might give him an advantage, a fresh pair of eyes. Who's to say you've been doing things right for 25 years?'

Alfonzo looked startled, as if he'd never considered that things could be done in any other way. 'Are you being serious?'

'Deadly,' replied the acrobat, fixing Alfonzo with an icy stare.

'Better than me? OK, I'll have a go,' agreed Alfonzo. 'But what exactly is "coaching"? I mean, they do it in sport, don't they?

'They certainly do. And your performers do it here at the circus. It's a way of getting people to perform at the peak of their abilities. But in business it's not a matter of simply telling people what to do. It's more a case of asking the right questions so that they start to think about what they're capable of.' Bruno glanced at Alfonzo, who was nodding enthusiastically. 'Let's take Jerry as an example. He is a bright lad but you're only tapping into a small percentage of his real capability. He's got a keen business brain but you're hardly using it at all. If you don't provide him with challenges he's probably going to get bored and leave. Why not give him some real responsibility? It's a great way to motivate and retain your staff. Coach him first, to enable him to grow into the role. Then take a week off and let him run the show.'

Alfonzo gulped. His face turned pale at the thought of anyone else running his show. 'You really mean it, don't you?'

The acrobat nodded reassuringly. 'Develop his skills, Alfonzo. If you want this business to grow, your people have to grow too. And Jerry's a great person to start with.'

By now crowds were thronging into the big top and the two men were lost in a mêlée of excited circus goers. At that moment, Jerry approached them through the crowd. 'Hey guys,' he smiled. 'Twenty minutes to go and you're sat here gassing. I've been looking everywhere for you. We were short by thirty chairs, so I sorted it with the acrobats and we've taken the spare ones from the wagon. We all mucked in. Everything's sorted. I hope that's OK?'

Alfonzo beamed from ear to ear. 'Perhaps inspiration does get these chairs sorted after all,' he mouthed to Bruno. 'Jerry,' he smiled. 'It's much more than OK. It's absolutely brilliant. And later, we're going to have a very positive chat about your future. I want to help you to grow young man. I want you to grow

into someone much better than I've ever been. I don't want you to make the same mistakes that I have…'

The two men sauntered away, Alfonzo with his arm draped around Jerry's shoulder, already passing on pearls of wisdom. Bruno watched as the men strode into the big top. He knew that the lesson had hit home.

Lesson 6

Any business is only as good as its employees. Invest as much time as possible in developing your people. Remember, leadership isn't about how high you can climb, but about how many people you can take with you. Coaching is a great way of drawing out true potential.

Questions to consider

1. Consider the best manager you've ever had and list their qualities.

2. How important were people to the manager's success?

3. How did you feel, working for that person?

4. Consider the worst person you've ever worked for. How did they treat people?

5. How did you feel, working for that person?

6. How do you think people feel working for you?

Challenge 10

Stop 'telling' and start 'coaching'. Think about how you communicate. Write down a series of positive questions that you can use at home and at work – ones that draw out a positive and thoughtful response. For example, instead of, 'How was your day?', rephrase and ask, 'What was the best thing about your day?' This will increase the likelihood of a positive response, thus getting the conversation off to a great start. Practise with your family, friends and work colleagues.

Challenge 11

Find out more about workplace coaching. Adopting a coaching style is much more difficult than it sounds, but is well worth investigating. Get yourself a life coach and become a coach yourself. Invest time in developing yourself and those around you.

Episode 7:

The massive goal principle

Alfonzo's circus continued on an upward spiral, inspired by the ringmaster's new-found leadership qualities. His new ways of thinking had become embedded in new habits and Alfonzo found that his default attitude was now positive and happy. He was proud that he was now thinking like the inspired 2% rather than the demoralised 98%. Sure, there were some significant challenges ahead, but the ringmaster found that they were more easily overcome with an optimistic mindset.

The best thing was how others were responding to the 'new' Alfonzo. His leadership style was raising everyone's game.

Bruno noticed the massive difference and decided to call on his boss one last time. He invited him out to lunch one quiet Tuesday when there was no performance and the two men wandered to a local pub. Bruno commented on the ringmaster's demeanour. 'You look younger, you sound passionate about raising standards and it must feel brilliant to be Alfonzo.'

'So true, my friend,' beamed the circus owner. 'And it's all turned around so quickly. I'm amazed at what's been achieved. I really don't know how to thank you.'

The acrobat grinned from ear to ear. 'Alfonzo, looking at you right now and seeing the staff perform

at their peak is all the thanks I require. But there is one more very important lesson. Perhaps the most important thing you have yet to learn.'

The ringmaster sat upright and engaged his brain. He was determined to soak up every word and practise his new listening skills. 'Tell me, young Maestro, what is this valuable final lesson?'

Bruno sipped his grapefruit juice. He placed the drink on the table and a large bumblebee landed on the edge of his glass and helped itself to a free drink. The men watched a while before Alfonzo waved his hand and flicked the insect away. 'Very interesting,' commented Bruno.

'What is?' asked the ringmaster.

'That bumblebee,' said Bruno, pointing, his finger following the insect as it buzzed into the distance. 'Did you know Alfonzo, that according to the laws of aerodynamics, a bumblebee can't fly. It is physically impossible. Look at its proportions. The bee's huge body can't possibly be propelled into the air by those tiny wings. Poor thing. It's not got a cat-in-hell's chance of flying.'

Not for the first time, Alfonzo furrowed his brow. 'Of course it can fly,' he laughed. 'I mean, it just did, didn't it?'

'Absolutely, my friend. It buzzes around oblivious to the fact that it's aerodynamically obsolete and scientifically defunct. Because crucially, nobody has told the bee that it can't fly! It isn't restrained by doubt or limiting beliefs. It just gets on with flying. I

guess this links with the final lesson. It's about goal setting, you see. It's about what you are trying to achieve with your circus and with your life.'

'Oh boy,' exclaimed Alfonzo, taking a couple of big swigs of beer. 'I guess my goal has always been to keep this circus ticking over as a going concern. I've always been too busy surviving to bother about proper goals.'

'I imagine survival has been a goal in itself,' smiled Bruno. 'But I think you're ready to think bigger. I want to share some more research with you. You may have heard of SMART objectives? They are often trotted out on business courses as the way to motivate people.'

Alfonzo nodded. 'Specific, Measurable, Achievable, Realistic and Time-Bound,' he chanted proudly.

'Yes, all that stuff,' dismissed Bruno. 'I don't believe in SMART objectives. They don't stretch people nearly enough. If your goals are "achievable" and "realistic" then you are just going to be average. Tell me, Alfonzo, can you think of one major achievement of human kind that would have been achieved if those concerned had set a SMART objective?'

Alfonzo grinned. 'I see your point,' he agreed. 'I guess we would never have gone to the moon or built the pyramids. And I suppose Mr Fosbury would never had invented his flop if he'd settled for being like everyone else.'

Bruno nodded. 'You see, all the examples you've given have gone way beyond SMART. They've resulted in big breakthroughs. The problem is, all

businesses set SMART objectives. That means that one business ends up thinking in just the same way as any other. They all end up being average. I would prefer you to aim for being world class. Accept nothing less.'

Alfonzo wanted desperately to be on board with his mentor's ideas, but was only half convinced. The furrows in his brow became deeper. 'But "world class" is absolutely huge!'

Bruno returned Alfonzo's stare. 'Exactly, my friend. That's why I prefer HUGGs: Huge Unbelievably Great Goals,' said the acrobat, holding his hands apart like an angler exaggerating the size of his catch. 'I want you to set yourself something that is massive – a world-class goal – and then go out and make it happen.'

Alfonzo fought his scepticism, the furrows remaining etched in his forehead. 'But with something so huge, where would I start?'

'I like to think of it as eating an elephant,' smiled Bruno. 'You wouldn't eat it in one go, but would have to break the challenge down into manageable chunks. Bit by bit, you would achieve your aim.' He smiled at Alfonzo's continued scepticism. 'Let me show you how. The very first thing is to come up with a Huge Unbelievably Great Goal. This has to be something that inspires you. Something you feel passionately about. Think of what this might be and then we'll work through your example. HUGGs can be personal or business goals. In positive psychology we sometimes call them "well-formed outcomes".

These are massive goals that you can see, hear and feel.'

'A massive goal that I can see, hear and feel,' repeated Alfonzo. His eyes were shining and he felt good. 'I guess we've already started something exciting here at the circus. What if I told you that I would like this group of performers to be the best in the world. Blimey, that's a pretty huge goal. That's a well-formed outcome because, in my mind's eye, I can picture it, hear it and feel it. The prospect excites me. Boy does it excite me!'

'Brilliant,' said Bruno. He opened the folder in front of him and withdrew a blank sheet of paper on which he drew a pyramid. At the top of the pyramid he wrote, 'To be the best performers in the world'.

'This, my friend, is your HUGG – your Huge Unbelievably Great Goal.' Bruno divided the pyramid into layers and then each layer into smaller blocks before passing the diagram and pencil to Alfonzo. 'See this bottom layer of blocks? These are your foundations. Your HUGG will only be achieved with solid foundations, so tell me what you have to do *right now* to begin to move towards your HUGG. What *habits* do you need to get into to create your bright future?'

Alfonzo picked up the pencil and thought out loud. 'I already have some of the habits,' he smiled. He began to write in some of the foundation blocks: 'be positive', 'coach and support', 'listen', 'invest in people', 'choose my attitude', 'lead by inspiration' and 'improve resources'.

'There, no prompting necessary. These are the things I know I have to do all day every day because without them we have no chance of being world class.'

'A great start,' encouraged Bruno. 'Now look at the next layer of the pyramid. Once these foundation habits are established, what do you have to do next to move towards your well-formed outcome?'

Alfonzo sat quietly and thought things through before writing: 'consult the teams', 'develop Jerry', 'fix the big top', 'get sponsorship' and 'keep going even when things don't work out'. He finished with a smile before moving on to the next layer of the pyramid, eventually finishing with a neat triangle, all boxes filled. Alfonzo swapped his pencil for his beer and took some satisfying swigs. 'If that bumblebee can fly, then so can this circus.'

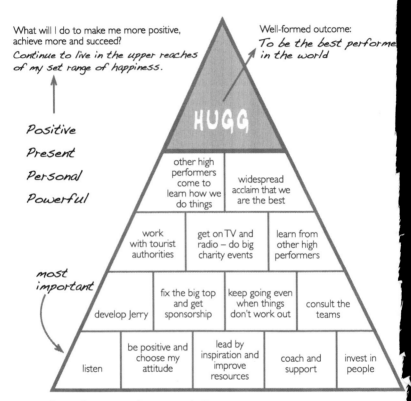

What will I do to make me more positive, achieve more and succeed?

Continue to live in the upper reaches of my set range of happiness.

Well-formed outcome:

To be the best performer in the world

Positive

Present

Personal

Powerful

HUGG

| other high performers come to learn how we do things | widespread acclaim that we are the best |

| work with tourist authorities | get on TV and radio – do big charity events | learn from other high performers |

most important

| develop Jerry | fix the big top and get sponsorship | keep going even when things don't work out | consult the teams |

| listen | be positive and choose my attitude | lead by inspiration and improve resources | coach and support | invest in people |

Personal statement: from now on I will…

make a conscious and sustained effort to…

The two men leaned over the finished pyramid.
'I love the Huge Unbelievably Great Goal,' said
Bruno. 'It is truly massive. But look at what you've
done. You've broken it down into bite-size,
manageable chunks. You are eating the elephant a bit
at a time. The point is that each of these chunks is
achievable. Therefore, if you achieve each one, your
HUGG will eventually become a reality. So where
are you going to start?'

Alfonzo ran his finger along the bottom of the
pyramid. 'I think I already have,' he beamed. 'There's
nothing unachievable on here. It's basically dead
simple. Rather than drifting, this pyramid will focus
my efforts. I guess I can cross each chunk off as I
achieve it. I can monitor progress. But it will still take
massive energy and effort, right?'

'Absolutely,' agreed Bruno. 'It will take massive effort,
because it's a massive goal. Drawing this diagram
doesn't achieve your goal, you do. This will help you
focus on what you want and give you some direction,
but you remain responsible for driving the whole
thing forward. Let me share some more thinking with
you. Most top achievers don't set realistic and
attainable goals. They think differently. Most set
HUGGs and then have the passion to follow through
on their dreams. The other thing that sets them apart
is that they absolutely do not give up… ever. It seems
to me, Alfonzo, that you have the HUGG, but do you
have the passion to follow it up, particularly when
things don't go according to plan?'

'Do I have the passion?' questioned the big man,
puffing out his chest and draining the last of his beer.
'Just you watch me go!'

Lesson 7

A Huge Unbelievably Great Goal should be one that
inspires you. You should be able to picture it, hear it
and feel it. Remember that top achievers set huge
goals. They also have the positive outlook that drives
them towards their HUGGs. They never give up.

Questions to consider

1. Think of a HUGG that you can apply to your
    personal and/or business life.

2. Imagine you have already achieved your HUGG.
    What do you see, hear and feel?

3. Break your HUGG down into manageable chunks.

4. Consider the habits that you need to put in place to
    move you in the right direction.

5. Consider who else you need to get on board to
    make your HUGG happen.

Challenge 12

Complete the following HUGG pyramid.
Once complete, share it with others
(maybe stick it on your fridge where you
will see it every day). Each day, do three
things that will move you towards your
ultimate goal.

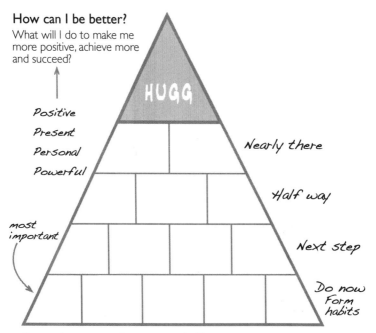

How can I be better?

What will I do to make me more positive, achieve more and succeed?

Positive
Present
Personal
Powerful

HUGG

Nearly there

Half way

most
important

Next step

Do now
Form
habits

Personal statement: from now on I will…

Episode 8:
Sharing the vision

The next few months were hectic. Normal circus activities continued, but Alfonzo made time to coach his young protégé and focus on the goal of achieving world-class performance. He made a conscious effort to ask the right questions and tease out Jerry's good ideas. Most were very simple yet had an enormous impact on the circus. Alfonzo found that Jerry was a natural with people. He was great with customers and performers and was a much better communicator than the ringmaster. Alfonzo watched as Jerry grew in confidence, and marvelled at the way he could express his ideas to the team. One of his ideas was to call a team meeting. 'What if the performers have lots of ideas too?' he asked. 'We need to develop them too, don't we?'

The very next morning, all training was cancelled. Alfonzo visited every caravan and asked all staff to report to the big top at 10am sharp. The rumour mill kicked into action and the word was that a special meeting had been called because the show was losing money. Special meetings – they never had any meetings, never mind special ones! There was unease among the assembled crowd as Alfonzo banged his cane on the table to quell the rumblings of the performers.

What followed was from the heart. Alfonzo hadn't planned anything, but the words just poured out, thankfully more or less in the order he wanted. He

thanked each and every member of staff for being so brilliant. He said that he was aware that in recent years the circus had lost focus and, as the ringmaster, he accepted responsibility for this. 'I've not been leading and I've certainly not been inspiring,' he admitted. 'And, worst of all, I've not been listening.' Alfonzo shook his head sadly. 'Ladies and gents,' he acknowledged. 'It pains me greatly, but I've stopped you being the best you can be, and I'm so sorry.'

The ringmaster paused and dabbed his brow. 'So sorry,' he sighed, looking at the breathless audience. 'But that's about to change,' he beamed through sparkling eyes. 'I want to enable you. I want to inspire you. And most of all I want to listen to how you think we can make this circus brilliant.' The circus staff were transfixed as their boss told them of the vision that he shared with Jerry. He painted a picture of future glory that surpassed anything he'd ever thought of before. Alfonzo felt energy pumping through his veins. He watched as eyes grew wider, the staff sharing his passion. 'It's about being world class,' he enthused. 'And it's not my vision, it's shared,' he explained excitedly. 'It's *ours*,' he urged, holding his hands aloft. 'And I need you to make it happen.' Alfonzo finished, not quite sure what reaction he'd get. He dabbed his brow nervously and looked at the assembled faces. For a moment there was silence, broken only by a sob from Angela the new trainee clown, obviously moved by Alfonzo's passion.

It was Jerry's turn. He cleared his throat. 'We have a great leader and a clear vision. Our dream is to

make this the best circus the world has ever seen.'
He followed this with two very simple questions,
'How can we work together to make this vision a
reality?' and 'How can we be brilliant?'

Silence prevailed once more. Then Merck, an
established acrobat, shouted, 'Well, we have lots of
ideas for improving our part of the act. Why don't
we all go away and work on our own areas, then
come back and present what we plan to do and how
fantastic it will be?'

There were murmurings of approval. 'Yes, then we
can decide how we can work together to make this
the best show on the planet,' offered Sheba the
unicyclist, clearly sharing the vision.

And that was that. Alfonzo was amazed at the
response Jerry's idea had produced. The following
day there was another full team meeting where each
group of performers outlined their plans for
improvement. It was decided that some performers
would retrain to help in other areas. Alfonzo sat
quietly and watched, prompting when needed but
making a conscious effort to listen, really listen, to
what was being said. He marvelled at the way Jerry
handled the meeting.

The next two months were manic. Extra training was
arranged and the performers revelled in their new
roles. Alfonzo found that there was a team of early
morning litter-pickers and that little jobs like filling
diesel generators were always done without him
having to ask. The entire team of performers went
into town and performed in the city centre, handing

out balloons and selling tickets for the shows. Audience levels rose to hitherto unheard of levels and there was a vibrancy about Alfonzo's circus that even surpassed that of the halcyon days. As the autumn season progressed and the rain clouds gathered no more umbrellas were needed – the hole in the roof somehow seemed to have mended itself! Alfonzo didn't know exactly who had done it or how, but he thanked the team at one of the regular meetings they now had. Long faces and arguments were replaced by smiles, laughter and cooperation.

The ringmaster noticed some interesting side effects of the 'New Alfonzo's'. For one thing, he wasn't having to continually recruit and train new performers. Staff were signing up for Alfonzo's, being trained up and staying! In fact, he even had a waiting list of new performers, ready to drop in if someone left, which they seldom did. Alfonzo himself started using his time to plan for the future: new acts, new towns, sponsorship agreements, each strategically thought out to give the circus a competitive advantage – he found himself being effective as well as efficient. He involved Jerry at every opportunity.

The performers decided that the final show of the year was to be a charity event with every penny going to disadvantaged children. Free tickets were issued to schools and major sponsorship was lined up. Alfonzo found himself on local TV and radio plugging the event. One of the TV reporters hailed Alfonzo's performers as 'among the best in the world'. Alfonzo's Huge Unbelievably Great Goal was inching closer. He and his team were bursting

with pride at the thought of actually putting something back into the community.

Then disaster struck.

It was late autumn, on the night before the charity show, the final performance of the season. It was a cold and rainy night but the performers hardly noticed, working late to make sure every detail was right for the following day. The big top was specially prepared, the sponsorship flags in place, even a big screen hired for the event. As the performers turned out their caravan lights, a small band of animal rights campaigners broke into the circus camp and set fire to the big top. The first Bruno knew about it was when he was woken at 2am by shouting outside. He pulled on his trousers and flung open the door, panic rising within, eyes wild at the scene before him. The night sky was aglow with orange, the flames creating an impressive show all of their own. The terrified screams of people and animals filled the air. A pyjama'd and barefoot Alfonzo also ran out into the nightmare, not knowing which way to turn – chaos in every direction. Everywhere people were running, some in terror, some trying to organise buckets of water to quench the flames. From that minute Alfonzo knew the big top was gone forever. It was already well ablaze, lighting up the scene of mayhem.

Lesson 8

Disaster will happen at some point in your life. It may happen several times! In this example it is the burning of the business. In your life it may be redundancy, illness or the passing away of a loved one. Positive psychology tells us that a key ingredient in today's turbulent world is 'resilience' or 'bouncebackability'. Even happy and positive people will face major challenges in life. They will inevitably have lows – but their resilience means they won't stay down for long.

Questions to consider

1. Is your glass half empty or half full?

2. How often do you initiate or join in a negative conversation (about the weather, traffic, government policy, repeats on TV…)?

3. Can you control the weather, traffic, government or repeats on TV?

4. Explain, therefore, why it's in your best interests to expend valuable energy getting worked up about them.

5. Consider how you'd feel if you reframed how you thought about some of the negatives in your life.

6. What positives are there in your life? List them.

7. How resilient are you (i.e. when things don't go according to plan, how quickly do you bounce back)?

8. How could you change your habits to become more resilient?

Challenge 13

'Reframing' is a technique that aims to combat negative thoughts and feelings. Ninety per cent of all British conversations start with a negative (usually about the weather or traffic!). Practise a positive conversation starter and a positive reply about the weather or the traffic (yes, I know this is difficult because we've had a lifetime of whinging about it!). Get into the habit of speaking positively, even when those around you aren't. This is a really interesting challenge to carry out. Monitor how you feel and gauge the response you get.

Warning note: Don't overdo the Pollyanna effect! Don't be so ridiculously positive that you annoy people – but consciously make an effort to see the good in the world and comment on it.

Episode 9:

The inevitability of bad times

Alfonzo returned to the scene two days later, having discharged himself from hospital (where he'd been taken for treatment of minor burns and smoke inhalation) against doctor's orders, catching a taxi to the outskirts of the town. The taxi driver had cheerfully commented on Alfonzo's terrible smoker's cough, an irony really as the ringmaster had never touched a cigarette in his life. But true, it was a smoker's cough of sorts.

He paid the driver and stepped out of the cab into the field, his feet immediately soaked by the early morning dew. It was a perfectly still morning, a fine mist covering the grass, the tranquillity of the scene an overwhelming contrast to that of two nights ago. Tears welled in his eyes as he surveyed the remnants of his once famous circus, his life's work, now a smouldering wreck.

The big top was totally destroyed, the central pole still upright but the charred remains of canvas hanging loose like a yacht's sails in the doldrums. Many of the caravans had also gone up in smoke and now looked like burned-out joyriders' wrecks. His caravan had survived, but in a way this grieved him most because scrawled in red paint across the side was a graffiti message, 'Animal killers go home'. This couldn't be further from the truth. Didn't these people know that most of the circus animals were rescued from cruelty and had been nursed back to full fitness by his team? The animals were always painstakingly and lovingly looked after.

Alfonzo walked silently through the desolate scene. The dawn chorus was as cheerful as ever, but how could it be? He saw one of Curly's polka-dot bow ties lying on the ground, picked it up and allowed himself a half-smile. What a shame for the clown, especially as he'd just trained everyone else up. How ironic that things had collapsed just as everything was beginning to fall into place. Thoughts flowed haphazardly; memories flooded his mind. Wasn't fate a bummer? Alfonzo's chest was tight from smoke inhalation and his breathing rattled. The proud ringmaster pulled a chair from the wreckage and sat on it, cradling his head in his bandaged hands, making no effort to stop the tears that engulfed him.

It was three months later that the postcard arrived. Alfonzo's son brought it to the breakfast table and handed it to his mother along with the assortment of credit card offers and bills. 'This one's for Dad, from a bloke called, looks like… Eddie Hassenthaler,' he read, squinting at the handwriting. 'Who's he?'

His mum seemed momentarily startled, then lost in thought. 'Hessenthaler?' she echoed. 'I think that's Curly's real name.' She put the postcard to one side until her husband came home.

Episode 10:

Staying positive in adversity

The postcard lay on the kitchen table until Alfonzo returned home after a weary day caretaking at the local junior school. It wasn't the job he wanted but there were bills to pay. And anyway, what does an ageing ringmaster do for a living when his life's work has burned away overnight? His CV was hardly loaded with qualifications.

Alfonzo turned the key and let himself into the small rented flat. Despite his predicament he had made a determined effort to stay cheerful. Bruno's lessons had stayed with him through these turbulent months and he sometimes wondered whether he'd have been able to cope without what he'd learned from him. Alfonzo kept coming back to something Bruno had said the very first time they'd met, before he had even hired the acrobat. 'Use the past as a library, not as a home,' he'd said, and Alfonzo was trying to do just that. He'd moved on – well, there was no choice really. But the more he considered his situation, the more choices he realised he had. Alfonzo had come to the conclusion that you can't escape stress and he'd become reconciled to the fact that life wasn't fair. There was no magic wand that could be waved to remove the chaos and drudgery of daily life, but choosing your attitude did help you to cope better with whatever life threw at you. Alfonzo considered he'd had more thrown at him in the last four months than most people have in a lifetime, yet he was still smiling. He was acutely aware of the choices he had. He could choose to withdraw into himself and

live miserably, infecting his friends and family with negativity, or he could choose to come out fighting, strong of spirit and purposeful of mind, charting his family through difficult waters. Through his musings with Bruno he was aware of choice, attitudes and the fact that he could still choose to be brilliant – even in adversity. So he'd taken the caretaker's job, as a stopgap at least, until something better turned up. What's more, he'd chosen to be a cheerful caretaker, a positive father and a brilliant husband.

Alfonzo walked into the kitchen to greet his wife. They embraced warmly before she pointed to the postcard on the table. 'Something from a Mr Hessenthaler,' she offered slightly reluctantly, not knowing how her husband would react.

'Mr Hessenthaler?' repeated Alfonzo, eyebrow raised. 'Why, there's only one Mr Hessenthaler that I know.' He picked up the postcard and read:

> To the greatest ringmaster of them all.
> You are cordially invited to witness the greatest show on earth, 8pm,
> Saturday 15 March,
> Westhampton Theatre
> > Best wishes
> > > Eddie Hessenthaller

Episode 11:

The value of empowered teams

March 15 was soon upon them and Alfonzo and his family boarded the evening train to Westhampton, intrigued by Curly's postcard. Alfonzo was puzzled by the whole affair. The circus performers had disbanded immediately after the fire – well, there was no point in hanging around as the circus was clearly finished. He wondered what had become of them, but because of the nature of travellers they had disappeared as quickly as they'd formed. He had tried to track some of them down as soon as he got out of hospital. He had a few mobile numbers but no forwarding addresses – after all, their caravans had burned so they had no addresses!

The picture became clearer as soon as he and his family stepped off the train in Westhampton. The first thing Alfonzo saw was a huge poster advertising 'The Greatest Show On Earth' at Westhampton Theatre, with tonight as the opening night of a two-week run. Alfonzo's heart skipped a beat. Could Curly really have organised the performers?

They left the station and followed the sign for the town centre. Towering above was another billboard, this time advertising 'Alfonzo's: Come And See The Best Performers In The World!' There was Curly's grinning face, 20 feet high, with the catchphrase 'Laugh like there's no tomorrow – today!'

There were a lot of people walking the streets of Westhampton, all drawn in the same direction, as if

a giant magnet was somehow pulling them along. As Alfonzo turned the corner he noticed that the main road was closed, with police redirecting the traffic. He saw a fun fair and a big screen with a sponsor's name emblazoned in neon. He saw merchandising stalls, he smelled candyfloss and baked potatoes. He heard laughter and chattering voices. He saw a huge swarm of people milling around the theatre, and as he got closer he became part of it. He heard hysterical canned laughter and saw a small boy with a Curly the Clown mask. 'Look at this,' he giggled. 'When I press this button the mask laughs like Curly,' demonstrating to his friend, the tinny laughter adding to the cacophony of sound.

Alfonzo was in a daze. His name was everywhere yet he wasn't part of it. How could Curly steal his name like this?

Alfonzo and his family entered the theatre and bought a programme. They found their seats, right at the back of the arena, and Alfonzo leafed through the glossy magazine. All the old acts seemed to be there, everyone had their own page with a brief biography – Alfonzo considered it to be very professional. There was even a web address and a list of towns where Alfonzo's show was scheduled to perform. There were some seriously big venues to be filled. There was a loyalty card as well as an invitation for children to come to clown open days. 'Paint a permanent smile on your face with Curly's Clown School', proclaimed the ad on page five. Alfonzo read on, enthralled. There were full-page corporate advertisements, Alfonzo merchandise, Christmas gifts and you could even book the

performers for your own private party. Page 11 screamed, 'Create the ultimate corporate training event with Alfonzo's', urging firms to book 'trapeze days' or 'clown events' for their staff. 'The perfect way to create trust, loyalty and teamwork.' Great idea. Alfonzo noticed that Jerry was listed as 'Business Development Manager'. 'The cheeky little so-and-so,' he muttered under his breath. 'Seems like he may have grown into boots that are too big for him.'

Alfonzo glanced up and surveyed the scene. He couldn't see a single empty seat or a child without some sort of Alfonzo merchandise. Eventually the lights dimmed and the curtain went up. There was Curly, not as a clown but as Eddie Hessenthaler, sitting on a chair in centre stage, head down, looking at his feet. Just an ordinary bloke. Moments passed; nothing happened; the moments built into an eternity. Gradually Eddie Hessenthaler raised his head to look at the expectant audience, his face serious and sad. There was no make-up, no magic, just plain old Eddie. He cleared his throat. 'Erm, ladies and gentleman,' he announced, slightly downcast, 'I have some bad news.' The crowd remained silent apart from an inadvertently pressed Curly mask that was laughing hysterically from the depths of the auditorium. The canned laughter eventually ceased and Eddie Hessenthaler continued, still downbeat. 'We have assembled the finest performers in the world for your show tonight. We are prepared to dazzle, amaze and delight you. But ladies and gentlemen, we are missing a vital ingredient, something very special, something essential to our success.'

Boys and girls looked at their mums and dads with puzzled faces and quizzical eyes. Is everything going to be all right? Mums and dads looked back, equally perplexed, with furrowed brows – not sure, but we hope so. Then Eddie Hessenthaler delivered the killer blow. 'We have nobody to link it all together. We have no compere. We have no ringmaster, so the show must be cancelled.'

There were gasps of amazement from the audience. The disappointment was palpable.

Eddie Hessenthaler rose from his chair and walked to the front of stage. He waited for hush, the consummate professional, Alfonzo nodding in approval from the back of the theatre. 'Unless, of course,' he boomed, 'we have a ringmaster in the house?'

Westhampton Theatre was packed. Among the assembled crowd were people from many occupations. There were 44 nurses, 12 doctors, 22 teachers, six bricklayers, four plumbers, seven architects, five dinner ladies, two binmen, six fire-fighters, eight shop assistants and an array of others too numerous to mention. Plus, of course, thousands of children. But there was only *one* ringmaster. Alfonzo rose from his seat and surveyed the scene, chest out, stomach in, broad grin lighting up his face.

Above the hubbub of the crowd he made himself heard. 'Excuse me, my dear friend,' he boomed from the back. 'I have some experience as a ringmaster.' Silence descended and necks craned to see who was

speaking. Alfonzo paused for effect, noticing hope in the children's eyes. 'Perhaps I can be of assistance? After all, I would hate these good people to miss out on the greatest night of their lives. If you will do me the honour, I would like to host your troop of talented performers.'

The moment of silence was followed by excited chatter. Who dared be so bold as to volunteer to lead the show? En masse, a sea of hopeful faces broke into smiles and hands joined together in tumultuous applause as Alfonzo galloped down the aisle and made his way onto the stage. He embraced Curly, whispering 'you sneaky so-and-so' into the clown's left ear. A box appeared from the wings and Alfonzo opened it to find his ringmaster's top hat and Union Jack waistcoat. He proudly fitted them and composed himself, choking back the emotion of the moment.

Then, and only then, could the show begin.

Episode 12:

Taking personal responsibility

It was truly the most magnificent of evenings. It wasn't until after midnight that the paying customers were finally persuaded to go home, reluctantly trudging away, many having booked for the following night. They could hardly wait to tell their families, friends, neighbours, school friends and workmates. It had been a truly awesome experience – everyone excelled and the ringmaster was pretty good considering that he'd been pulled from the audience!

Calm eventually prevailed and Alfonzo gathered the performers on stage. 'Well, my friends,' he beamed, 'that was the most incredible night of my life and the lives of the 3000 people lucky enough to be present. Never have I seen such a fabulous and seemingly effortless show. Curly, your clowns are the funniest ever, and you, young lady, are the best tightrope walker we've ever had,' he beamed at the trainee, whose face lit up at the praise. 'What did I say? Told you you had star quality, didn't I?'

'We owe it all to you, Alfonzo,' said Jerry from the back. 'You inspired us to do it, you encouraged us to change the act. Together we decided that what we had was worth keeping. Who needs a big top when you've got talent and teamwork like ours? We've booked theatres around the UK and we're determined to keep improving what we do. We need you at the helm.'

'Fantastic,' smiled Alfonzo. 'But you don't owe me a thing. I haven't achieved this, *you have*. I haven't changed you, *you have*. I haven't created this fabulous show, *you have*. I just created the environment in which you could improve – but you did the improving.'

Alfonzo looked at the assembled crowd. There was one face missing, in fact he'd been missing from the show as well. 'Where's Bruno?' enquired the ringmaster. 'Where's my flexible friend?'

Curly piped up. 'I'm afraid he's gone, Gaffer. Said his work was done here and he was needed elsewhere. Said every factory, shop, business, school and family needed him. We tried to persuade him to stay but he jacked it in and walked. He said you'd understand. He said to give you this,' said the clown, passing a sealed brown envelope to the ringmaster.

Alfonzo pocketed the envelope and looked around at the beaming faces. He felt an overwhelming passion for life. Now he really did understand. He calculated that he had about 12 000 days left and every one of them was going to be brilliant. 'He's right,' conceded Alfonzo, feeling warmth within, 'his job here is done.'

It was the early hours of Sunday morning by the time Alfonzo got home. He kissed his wife goodnight and retired to the kitchen. He flicked the kettle on. He was exhausted but on too much of a high to contemplate sleep. The big man smiled as he pulled the envelope from his coat pocket. He slid his finger

under the flap and pulled out a sheet of A4. He nodded as he read:

> For a long time it had seemed to me that life was about to begin — real life. But there was always some obstacle in the way, something to be got through first, some unfinished business, time still to be served, or a debt to be paid. Then life would begin. At last it dawned on me that these obstacles were my life.'
>
> Alfred D'Souza

The final lesson:

How many days do you have left? The truth is that you don't know, but how many do you want to waste? Take the lessons and apply them. Don't try to be anyone else, just be yourself, brilliantly!

Question to consider

1. Who are you at your best?

2. Do you want to be in the negative 98% or the positive 2%? Why?

3. What areas of your life do you need to change?

4. What's stopping you from changing them?

Challenge 14

Be yourself, brilliantly. Change your emphasis from 'leading by example' to 'leading by inspiration', at work and at home.

Challenge 15

Adopt the habit of appreciating what you have, rather than grumbling about what you don't have. Wake up! It's a much better place to be.

Challenge 16

Stop comparing yourself with others. Compare yourself with you. How can you be a better version of you tomorrow, and the next day, and the next? Don't just think about it. Do it.

Section 3:

The encore

Transformational leadership

I so wanted to avoid writing an academic text. People who write academia must be so clever to understand all those theories of management, leadership, teams, change and communication. Textbooks are crammed full of interesting information, case studies and quotes from people I know I should have heard of. But I guess that's the point, they are faintly interesting but hardly challenging. A textbook has never inspired me to change, but people have.

Being Brilliant is actually bursting with leadership messages but they are just not written academically. If leadership really is about 'lighting fires within people', then Alfonzo learned the lesson and applied it. He became a leader by creating an environment where people could excel. If you think about it, he didn't actually tell anyone what to do or how to do it – they already knew how to be brilliant, all he did was get them to believe it and inspire them into action. In short, Alfonzo became an 'enabler'. He changed from 'leading by example' to 'leading by inspiration', developing his people on the way. Textbooks would call this 'transformational leadership' or 'getting people to do things because they want to do them' (rather than 'transactional leadership', which is essentially getting people to do things because you've told them that they have to).

The differences between 'transactional' and 'transformational' are fundamental to modern leadership. Competitive pressures mean we must get our teams to go one step further than we've ever

needed them to go before. And tomorrow we need them to take another step forward, then another, and another… Will they grudgingly take that extra step because we tell them that they have to? Or will they willingly go the extra mile because they trust you and share your passion? In the end, the second option is the only sustainable way forward, yet it is the most difficult to facilitate. Achieve this and you have achieved transformation.

However, transformational leadership is only part of the success equation. I believe that modern organisations need to have all the ingredients of the formula below:

$$IQ + EQ + HUGG \overset{TFL}{=} MaD$$

In fact, this formula is the backbone of *Being Brilliant*. Alfonzo has been through it, and the challenge is for you to apply it to your life. Unfortunately it isn't a magic formula. It's not one where we can wave a magic wand and everything falls neatly into place. It involves a great deal of hard work. For many individuals it means a significant element of personal change. For organisations it invariably requires a refocus on some core essentials – its people! Some organisations may never make it because the cultural barriers are too massive.

Let's consider each element in turn.

Most people are already familiar with the term IQ. It is your 'intelligence quotient'. If you like, it's how 'clever' you are. How many exams did you pass? What is your intellect? Can you solve problems and

think on your feet? How dextrous is your mind? In the modern, ultra-competitive world you need to make sure your CV is as strong as it can be, so investment in qualifications is very important. Companies need people who are switched on between their ears. Of course, learning nowadays is a lifelong challenge. I don't say this glibly. For most people, business life is less like an ocean cruise and more like white water rafting, so we have no choice but to move with the times. You will have noticed that it's a crazy world out there. There's no room for complacency. In order to maintain a competitive edge, we must continue to absorb information at ever increasing rates. Your brain power is therefore crucial.

Ask yourself, what are you doing to stay ahead of the competition? What are you doing to boost your brain power? How can you make sure you continue to learn?

Nowadays, companies are looking for more than traditional 'intelligence' as measured by your IQ. They need people with high EQ. This is your 'emotional quotient', sometimes called your 'emotional intelligence' or, even sexier, 'emotional literacy'. In its simplest interpretation, this is your people skills. EQ remains a relatively new area of study, but is vital to understanding yourself and getting the best out of those around you. It's about knowing which buttons to press, in yourself and other people, in order to get the very best. How do we turn the dial to 'maximum potential'? How can we 'tune in' to others, get on their wavelength? If we can learn this elusive set of 'intelligences' then we

can create rapport, thus improving the quality of our personal relationships. This impacts on all aspects of life – both in and out of work.

So, once again I would ask you to consider whether you are sufficiently 'tuned in' to your fellow human beings. Your work colleagues, customers and manager. And what about your friends, children and partner? Crucially, how can you improve your emotional intelligence? Alfonzo learned to see, hear and feel the world from another perspective and to appreciate that others' views of the world may be radically different from his. These views are not wrong, just different. Everyone has what textbooks would call 'maps of the world'. Your map comprises the knowledge and experience that you accumulate as you go through life, building your very own picture of the world that's unique. EQ requires us to understand that everyone's map is different, and to appreciate this uniqueness of knowledge and experience. Understanding where people are coming from gives you a better chance of a relationship. And it's these relationships that are crucial to building world-class teams, loyal customers, successful marriages and harmonious family units. Alfonzo also learned that you can only create relationships by finding time to listen, understand and coach. Often, in the hurly burly of the modern world, we don't give enough time to our people – either in or out of work!

Even so, having a high IQ and EQ is no guarantee of success. We need to set ourselves some Huge Unbelievably Great Goals. These will give you long-term focus as well as a framework to move in the

right direction. If your HUGG is your destination, the pyramid is your map and positive action is your journey. With a little coaching, Alfonzo got there in the end.

Have you got a HUGG? Is it framed correctly (i.e. can you clearly see, hear and feel it)? If you haven't got a HUGG, do you need one? Start to think of a one-, three- and five-year plan. Your brain is a fabulous piece of technology. It has a built-in radar called your Reticular Activating System (RAS), which automatically filters the world around you. It's your very own lens. Your RAS notices things that are important to you and blocks out things that aren't. For example, you immediately notice all the cars that are the same make and model as yours. Like magic, your RAS brings them to your attention. If you are thinking of selling your house, you will immediately see 'for sale' signs everywhere. Your RAS also homes in on goals. If you have a HUGG, your mind will filter the world and help you notice things that are crucial to achieving your end result. No goal means no filter and therefore no focus. Individuals need goals, as do teams, businesses and families.

TFL stands for 'TransFormational Leadership'. You will be painfully aware that merely setting goals doesn't necessarily mean you will achieve them. HUGGs are only as powerful as the leadership that drives them. HUGGs with no leadership remain as dreams. Without transformational leadership HUGGs become Huge 'Unachievable' Great Goals. The stronger your transformational leadership, the more likely you are to achieve your goal. TFL is

about being proactive and making things happen, rather than sitting in your comfort zone waiting for life to ignite. You must take responsibility for lighting the blue touch paper yourself! To bring it back to you again, consider (honestly) whether your drive and enthusiasm could be more intense. Or more focused. Or both. Have you lit your blue touch paper? Are you inspiring yourself to action? Are you a positive presence for others? Do you get the best out of your work colleagues, your family, your team? What else can you do to improve your knowledge and understanding of transformational leadership that will help you move to the next level?

Put IQ, EQ, HUGG and TFL together and you will achieve 'MaD'. You will 'Make a Difference', not only to your life, but to those around you. This is therefore one of the few books that encourages you to go stark, raving MaD. Quite frankly, the madder you go the better!

The 'Big 5'

It's estimated that about 98% of the population exists way below their optimum levels of positivity and happiness. The remaining 2% are doing things differently, existing towards the upper level of how fantastic they can feel. They have boundless energy, optimism and passion for life. Their enthusiasm is as infectious as their smile. Having read countless books and reams of academic articles on 'positive psychology', it appears to me, in my simple world, that there are only five things that positive people do that the negative majority don't. Here are the 'Big 5' in all their glorious simplicity:

1 Positive people CHOOSE to be positive

They don't end up positive by accident, they actually choose to think positive thoughts, choose positive language and have a bright, sunny, upbeat manner. This is the biggest point of the Big 5, hence its number 1 position. If you don't do this one, you can forget the other 4!

Let me say the first of the Big 5 again, it's worth repeating. 'Positive people choose to be positive.' OK, I know it sounds ridiculously simple! I'm betting you're already aware of this fact. My question to you is, 'Are you consistently doing it? Or are you, like the 98% majority, failing to make any choice about how you feel, letting events dictate your day?' I don't want you just to be aware of the fact that you can make the choice to be positive – I want you to actually make the choice and physically make the changes that come with it. It's the most powerful choice you have.

2 Understand your impact

Most people vastly underestimate the influence they have on those around them. The positive 2% are more emotionally intelligent because they understand that they have a profound impact on those around them. The impact is in direct proportion to the closeness of the relationship – meaning that you are having a massive influence on family, friends, work colleagues and anyone else you come into frequent contact with. Believe me, your impact is massive. You can use it to inspire people or make them feel rubbish. Either way, you're having an impact. Are you consistently making the right call? What can you do to maximise your positive impact? Do you smile enough? Do you thank people? Do you give enough praise to your colleagues, children, partner and team? When did you last catch someone doing something really well and thank them for it? Any or all of these will immediately raise your positive impact.

3 Set huge goals

I must admit, I questioned this one. I thought long and hard about how setting goals could actually make people more positive and happy. I really struggled with it. Ultimately though, I guess it's fairly simple. The 98% negative majority don't set goals. They roll out of bed in the morning with the aim of surviving another day, probably counting down to the weekend. Hopefully tomorrow will be better. Whereas the positive 2% get out of bed with more focus. They have goals that give them direction. They know where they're aiming and that gives them a

spring in their step. Knowing where they want to get to gives them a better chance of taking positive action that will help them to get there.

4 'Bouncebackability' or resilience

To me, this is the most difficult of the Big 5. I would be in cloud cuckoo land if I said you could be positive and happy all day, every day. I mean, life's just not like that, is it? Everyone has dips. At some point, life is going to deal you such a blow that being happy and positive is impossible, inappropriate and irrelevant. Having a bad day is part of being human. So it's official – even positive people have lows. But, interestingly, they have reserves of optimism that mean they bounce back much more quickly. Their radar looks for reasons to bounce back to being positive, rather than for reasons to continue to be low. As I said, a difficult one to put into action, especially if life has dealt you a horrendous set of circumstances. But this resilience is vital to a sustained positive outlook. After all, there are so many things in everyday life that have the potential to get us down, that bouncebackability is a must (and, yes, it is a real word!).

5 Take personal responsibility

Three little words, but so much meaning. The brilliant 2% take personal responsibility for their feelings and lives. If things aren't working out, they change something about themselves to achieve a different result. Crucially, they don't vegetate, feel sorry for themselves or blame other people or

'circumstances' for being less than brilliant. In fact, they don't point the finger at anyone but themselves. Textbooks and psychologists call this 'self-efficacy' or an 'internal locus of control'. Translated, this means they take charge of their lives, believing that what they do really matters to their future outcomes. A positive today is very likely to generate a positive tomorrow. Another astonishingly simple point, but how many people do you know who sit through life in victim mode, blaming just about everything but themselves?

The questions are, 'What do you need to change about yourself to achieve a better result in life? Who or what do you blame when things don't go your way? Who's really responsible for the way your life turns out?' When it's written so starkly, I guess the answer is obvious.

So, five things that positive people do. And they do them consistently. There is a whole host of environmental factors that impact on personal wellbeing (e.g. your health), but I stand by the Big 5 as the key things that will really make a difference. Blindingly simple? Absolutely. Can you do them, starting today? It's your choice.

Artificial Intelligence?

In textbook land they talk of the theories of Maslow, Adair and Herzberg. All well and good, but these ideas are 30, 40 and 50 years old. Transformational leaders understand that leadership is about emotion. In fact, ultimately it is emotion that creates motion. Translated, this means that the way we feel drives our behaviour. Can we teach 'emotion'? Can we teach people how to inspire others? These are big questions that demand a book all of their own, but the simple answer is an unequivocally fence-sitting 'probably'!

I have worked for managers in the past whom I would call 'emotionally tone deaf'. They hadn't a clue how to inspire me and, even if they did know, they probably didn't care. They were far from brilliant at work and, guess what, they were equally insipid out of work. They were intelligent people (academically that is), but there was something missing. That 'something' was passion for life and, with it, the ability or desire to inspire those around them. They had a track record of academic intelligence but a dismal lack of emotional intelligence. To me such managers display 'artificial intelligence'; they are intellectually bright but emotionally dim. They have forgotten how to light their own internal fires, never mind anyone else's!

Modern life is fast, challenging and exhausting. The easiest thing is to let the pace of life knock the stuffing out of you. Before we know it we're 40 years old, then 50, then 60, then 70... and we look back on decades of missed opportunity. Our careers

might have progressed and we may have cash in the bank, but have we spent time enjoying the moments or have the moments passed us by?

You may have guessed that I'm not from the academic school of leadership thinking. I am very much from the 'doing' end of the spectrum. Don't get me wrong, words and theories are great. I love them. But only if they engage my energy. Happy, positive, passionate people don't talk about brilliance, they eat, sleep and breathe it. It's demonstrated in their words and also in their actions. So, my challenge to you is to consider the concepts, get yourself booked onto an 'Art of Being Brilliant' workshop and begin your plan of action. Not next year, not next month or next week. Not even tomorrow. Right now.

Let me finish with one massive thought. In the grand scheme of things, as our planet hurtles through space, spinning on its axis, we are completely and utterly insignificant dots of life flickering on a tiny rock, lost among billions of other tiny rocks in the solar system. On this grand scale our lives are over in the blink of an eye. In this scenario, our insignificance is staggering. But to all those we live and work with (and our children in particular) we are incredibly significant because we form part of their world. We are shaping their character, forming their belief systems and affecting their quality of life. Boy, are we significant!

For our sake and theirs let's make the effort to be brilliant. We only get one go at this life and if we don't at least make the effort, what's the point? It's your call.

Favourite quotes

On change:

'To avoid having the rug pulled from under your feet you must learn to dance on a shifting carpet.'

(Prof. John Quelch)

'In times of change, the learners will inherit the earth while the knowers will find themselves beautifully equipped to deal with a world that no longer exists.'

(Eric Hoffer)

On goals:

'There are two ways to die. You can stop breathing or you can stop dreaming.'

(taken from The Naked Leader Experience *by David Taylor)*

On the stress of modern life:

'Life is less like an ocean cruise and more like white water rafting.' *(Elif Olsen)*

On self-improvement:

'The ability to learn faster than your competitors will be the only sustainable competitive advantage of the future.'

(Arie de Gus)

On whether you are bold enough to change:

'One does not discover new lands without first consenting to lose sight of the shore for a very long time.'

(Andre Gide)

For those moments when you think you can't:

'Pooh, if you ever need me and I'm not around, you must remember this: You're braver than you believe and stronger than you seem and cleverer than you think.'

(A. A. Milne)

Further reading – *easy*

No big words, clear messages and lots of fun.

Fish by Stephen Lundin (Coronet Books, 2002)

SUMO by Paul McGee
(Capstone Publishing Ltd, 2005)

Feel the Fear and do it Anyway by Susan Jeffers
(Arrow, 1991)

The Naked Leader Experience by David Taylor
(Bantam, 2004)

The Pig of Happiness by Edward Monkton
(Harper Collins, 2004)

How to be Happy by Liz Hoggard
(BBC Books, 2005)

The Mind Gym (Time Warner, 2005)

Positively Happy by Noel Edmonds
(Vermilion, 2006)

Did You Spot the Gorilla? by Richard Wiseman
(Arrow, 2004)

Change Your Life in Seven Days by Paul McKenna
(Bantam Press, 2003)

The Little Soul and the Sun by Neale Donald Walsch
(Hampton Roads Publishing Co, 1998)

Further reading - *intermediate*

Stodgy in places, occasional big words, more academic but generally on message with Being Brilliant.

The 7 Habits of Highly Effective People by Stephen Covey (Simon & Shuster Ltd, 1999)

The New Leaders by Daniel Goleman (Time Warner, 2003)

The One Thing You Need to Know by Marcus Buckingham (Simon & Shuster Ltd, 2005)

Mans Search for Meaning by Victor Frankl (Wharton School Publishing, 2005)

Any books by Anthony Robbins

Further reading - *difficult*

Medicinal. Not nice to read but you feel they must be doing you some good. Can be heavy going, takes the messages further but uses big words to do so, for those who are very serious about wanting to know more about the underlying themes of Being Brilliant.

Authentic Happiness by Martin Seligman
(Nicholas Brealey Publishing Ltd, 2003)

Learned Optimism by Martin Seligman
(Pocket Books, 1998)

Working with Emotional Intelligence by Daniel Goleman (Bloomsbury Publishing plc 1999)

The Power of Appreciative Inquiry by Whitney and Trosten Bloom (Berrett-Koehler, 2003)

The Resilience Factor by Karen Reivich
(Random House, 2003)

The NLP Coach by Ian McDermott and Wendy Jago (the simplest NLP starter, but still laced with difficult terminology) (Piatkus Books, 2002)

The Power of Spirit by Harrison Owen
(Berrett-Koehler, 2000)